THIS PAGE INTENTIONALLY LEFT BLANK

INTRODUCTION

The National Interoperability Field Operations Guide (NIFOG) is a technical reference designed to support incident communications. This version marks the 14th year for the NIFOG. The NIFOG is updated on a regular basis and is a compilation of communication references and information that have been recommended by public safety practitioners across the country. Due to the increasing technical and regulatory nature of incident communications and information technology, it is, and will remain a work in progress. New content in 2.01 includes references on Information Technology, Emergency Wireless Carrier Services, Interference Management, Encryption, and Cybersecurity.

If you are not familiar with interoperability and mutual aid communications, start with the "How to Use the National Interoperability Field Operations Guide" section and recommend the reader become familiar with the tools available in this guide.

Your comments and input are encouraged and welcome at:
NIFOG@cisa.dhs.gov

Thank you,

Billy Bob Brown, Jr.
Executive Assistant Director for Emergency Communications
Cybersecurity and Infrastructure Security Agency

To download or request copies of the NIFOG, please visit
cisa.gov/safecom/field-operations-guides

Names of commercial products and services may be trademarks of their respective owners. Use of such names herein does not imply endorsement by CISA or the U.S. Government.

TABLE OF CONTENTS

HOW TO USE THE NATIONAL INTEROPERABILITY FIELD OPERATIONS GUIDE

What is the *National Interoperability Field Operations Guide*?

The *National Interoperability Field Operations Guide* (NIFOG) is a pocket-sized listing of land mobile radio (LMR) frequencies that are often used in disasters or other incidents where radio interoperability is required, and other information useful to emergency communicators developed by the Cybersecurity and Infrastructure Security Agency (CISA).

Terms used in this document:

- **FCC** – Federal Communications Commission
- **FCC Rules** – contained in Title 47, Code of Federal Regulations (47 CFR)
- **Federal** – used herein to differentiate between radio stations of the United States Government and those of any territorial; state, local, tribal, and territorial (SLTT), or regional government authority. "Federal Frequencies" refer to frequencies (channels) available for assignment to U.S. Government Agencies. Although the FCC is a Federal Government agency, the frequencies it administers are not "federal frequencies"- they are administered for SLTT governments, commercial entities, and individuals.
- **NPSTC** – the National Public Safety Telecommunications Council is a federation of organizations whose mission is to improve public safety communications and interoperability through collaborative leadership. NPSTC channel names used in the NIFOG are based on the latest version of the "Standard Channel Nomenclature for the Public Safety Interoperability Channels", APCO ANS 1.104.2-2017, approved January 3, 2017 by the American National Standards Institute (ANSI).
- **NRPC** – National Regional Planning Council is a collaborative network consisting of both 700 MHz & 800 MHz public safety Regional Planning Committees as established by the Federal Communications Commission. nrpc.us
- **NTIA** – National Telecommunications and Information Administration
- **NTIA Manual** – The NTIA "Manual of Regulations and Procedures for Federal Radio Frequency Management" ntia.doc.gov/

How is the NIFOG used?

The NIFOG may be used as a reference by radio technicians when programming channels in radios. It is recommended having these channels programmed in radios at all times, as permitted by the applicable regulations, rather than waiting until a disaster is imminent or occurring to do the programming.

The NIFOG is a useful tool for emergency communications planners, providing them with information on the interoperability channels most likely to be in the radios of responders from another discipline or jurisdiction.

The NIFOG is a useful tool for information technology specialists, as well, providing them with common references and information related to networking infrastructure and cybersecurity.

Do I need a license for these channels before programming them into radios?

If you are licensed under Part 90 of the FCC rules, you may program frequencies (other than maritime or aviation) that you are not licensed to use IF "the communications involved relate directly to the imminent safety-of-life or property" or "with U.S. Government stations ... in connection with mutual activities" (see FCC rules §90.25, §90.427 and §90.417). See "Conditions for Use of Federal Interoperability Channels", pages 19-22. There are no restrictions on programming frequencies into U.S. Government radios.

However, note that §90.403(g) requires that "[f]or transmissions concerning the imminent safety-of-life or property, the transmissions shall be suspended as soon as the emergency is terminated." Also, the safety of life provision of §90.417(a) makes it clear that the exception applies only when the communications involved "relate directly" to the "imminent" safety of life or property.

How can I use these frequencies if I do not have a license for them?

There are seven ways you can legally use these radio frequencies:

1. You or your employer may already have an FCC license or a NTIA authorization for some of the interoperability and common mutual aid channels.

2. **For FCC licensees**, the VHF, UHF, 700 MHz, and 800 MHz non-Federal National Interoperability Channels (e.g., VCALL10, VTAC11-14, UCALL40, UTAC41-43, the 700MHz interoperability channels, 8CALL90, and 8TAC91-94) are covered by a "blanket authorization" from the FCC - "Any Part 90 public safety eligible entity holding a Part 90 license may operate hand-held and vehicular mobile units on these channels without needing a separate authorization." – See §90.20(i). When North of Line A or East of Line C the blanket authorization in paragraph 90 of FCC R&O 00-348 applies only to mobile (including hand-held) stations operating with an effective radiated power (ERP) of 3 watts or less. At higher power levels, frequency coordination is required, see FCC Public Notice DA-09-1064, released May 13,2009. Line A and C are defined in 47CFR §90.7. You can check a location for Line A and Line C restrictions at wireless.fcc.gov/uls/index.htm?job=line_a_c.

3. You may operate on frequencies authorized to another licensee when that licensee designates you as a unit of their system, in accordance with FCC rule §90.421; or as an authorized user of a shared radio system pursuant to a written agreement as described in FCC rule §90.179.

4. In extraordinary circumstances, the FCC may issue a "Special Temporary Authority" (STA) for such use in a particular geographic area.

5. In extraordinary circumstances, the NTIA may issue a "Temporary Assignment" for such use in a particular area.

6. **If you are an FCC Part 90 licensee, you _may_ operate a mobile station on the Federal Interoperability Channels only when authorized by the FCC (by license or STA) and only for interoperability with Federal radio stations authorized by the NTIA to use those channels. See §90.25. You _may not_ use these channels for interoperability with other state, tribal, regional, or local radio stations – these are not a substitute for your regular mutual aid channels. See FCC Public Notice DA 01-1621, released July 13, 2001.**

7. When necessary for the IMMEDIATE protection of life or property, FCC Part 90 licensees may use prudent measures beyond the specifics of their license. See FCC rule §90.407, "Emergency communications." U.S. Government stations are authorized by NTIA rule 7.3.6 to utilize any frequency authorized to a non-federal radio station, under Part 90 of the FCC Rules and Regulations, when such use is necessary for communications with the authorized non-federal stations and is directly related to the emergency at hand. Such use is subject to the following conditions:

   - The non-federal licensee has given verbal or written concurrence;
   - Operations are conducted in accordance with the FCC Rules and Regulations;
   - Use is restricted to the service area and station authorization of the licensee;
   - All operations are under the direct control of the licensee and shall be immediately terminated when directed by the licensee;
   - Operations do not exceed 60 days; and,
   - The federal agency shall provide, through the agency's FAS representative to the FCC as soon as practicable, a written report of each such use.

FCC Rules and Regulations

Title 47   Code of Federal Regulations, Chapter I, Parts 0-199

              Electronic Code of Federal Regulations (eCFR)

   Part 80   Stations in the Maritime Services

              - for information on VHF Marine channels, see
                navcen.uscg.gov/?pageName=mtVhf

   Part 87   Aviation Services

   Part 90   Private Land Mobile Radio Services

   Part 95   Personal Radio Services (includes GMRS, FRS, CB, & MURS)

   Part 97   Amateur Radio Service

NTIA Rules and Regulations

Title 47   Code of Federal Regulations, Chapter III, Parts 300-399

   Part 300   Manual of Regulations and Procedures for Federal Radio
              Frequency Management (Redbook)

FCC Rules for Interoperability

§90.20(i) Nationwide Interoperability Channels.

The nationwide interoperability and mutual aid channels are listed below for the VHF..., UHF, 700 MHz and 800 MHz bands. (See §90.20(d)(80), §90.531(b)(1), §90.617(a)(1)... Any Part 90 public safety eligible entity holding a Part 90 license may operate hand-held and vehicular mobile units on these channels without needing a separate authorization. Base stations or control stations operating on these channels must be licensed separately: Encryption may not be used on any of the interoperability or mutual aid calling channels.
[62 FR 18845, Apr. 17, 1997]

*Note - AES Encryption permitted on all but the two nationwide interoperability calling channels. Must have accessible switch or other readily accessible control that permits the radio user to disable encryption.
47 CFR §90.553

§90.25 Non-Federal use of the Federal interoperability channels.

The Commission may authorize non-Federal licensees to operate mobile and portable radio units on the frequencies listed..., provided the applicant includes with its application to the Commission, written concurrence from the Statewide Interoperability Coordinator (SWIC) or state appointed official stating that the application conforms to the agreement with a federal agency with a valid assignment from the National Telecommunications and Information Administration.
[83 FR 19980, May 8, 2018]

§90.407 Emergency communications.

The licensee of any station authorized under this part may, during a period of emergency in which the normal communication facilities are disrupted as a result of hurricane, flood, earthquake or similar disaster, utilize such station for emergency communications in a manner other than that specified in the station authorization or in the rules and regulations governing the operation of such stations. The Commission may at any time order the discontinuance of such special use of the authorized facilities.
[49 FR 36376, Sept. 17, 1984]

§90.411 Civil defense communications.

The licensee of any station authorized under this part may, on a voluntary basis, transmit communications necessary for the implementation of civil defense activities assigned such station by local civil defense authorities during an actual or simulated emergency, including drills and tests. The Commission may at any time order the discontinuance of such special use of the authorized facilities. [49 FR 36376, Sept. 17, 1984]

§90.417 Interstation communication.

a)   Any station licensed under this part may communicate with any other station without restriction as to type, service, or licensee when the communications involved relate directly to the imminent safety-of-life or property.
b)   Any station licensed under this part may communicate with any other station licensed under this part, with U.S. Government stations, and with foreign stations, in connection with mutual activities, provided that where the communication involves foreign stations prior approval of the Commission must be obtained, and such communication must be permitted by the government that authorizes the foreign station.

§90.421 Operation of mobile station units not under the control of the licensee.

Mobile stations, as defined in §90.7, include vehicular-mounted and handheld units. Such units may be operated by persons other than the licensee ...

§90.423 Operation on board aircraft.

Allowed on most public safety frequencies up to 1-mile altitude, up to 10 watts, secondary to land-based systems; for air-to-mobile, air-to-base, air-to-air, and air-to-ship communications.

§90.427 Precautions against unauthorized operation.

... (b) Except for frequencies used in accordance with §90.417, no person shall program into a transmitter frequencies for which the licensee using the transmitter is not authorized.

NTIA Rules for Interoperability

7.3.4 Emergency Communications for which an Immediate Danger Exists to Human Life or Property

1. In situations where immediate danger exists to human life or property, an agency may operate temporarily on any regularly assigned frequency in a manner other than that specified in the terms of an existing assignment. Emergency operations under such situations should continue only as long as necessary to ensure that the danger to human life or property no longer exists. Emergency operations under these circumstances shall be reevaluated on a regular basis until such time as normal/routine operations can be reestablished.

2. Interoperable communications for disaster/emergency response involving federal, state, local, and tribal entities shall be in conformance with Section 4.3.16 of the NTIA. Additional information regarding interoperable communications can also be found in the National Interoperability Field Operations Guide (NIFOG) ... promulgated by the Department of Homeland Security.

7.3.6 Emergency Use of Non-Federal Frequencies

In emergency situations, a federal radio station may utilize any frequency authorized to a non-federal radio station, under Part 90 of the FCC Rules and Regulations, when such use is necessary for communications with non-Federal stations and is directly related to the emergency at hand.

Such use is subject to the following conditions:

a. The non-federal licensee has given verbal or written concurrence.

b. Operations are conducted in accordance with the FCC Rules and Regulations.

c. Use is restricted to the service area and station authorization of the licensee.

d. All operations are under the direct control of the licensee and shall be immediately terminated when directed by the licensee.

e. Operations do not exceed 60 days.

f. A written report of each such use shall be provided, through the agency's FAS [Frequency Assignment Subcommittee, of NTIA's IRAC (Interdepartment Radio Advisory Committee)] representative, to the FCC as soon as practicable.

7.5.2 Frequencies Authorized by the FCC for Ship Stations

Frequencies authorized by the FCC for ship stations may be used by Federal mobile stations to communicate with non-Federal stations in the maritime mobile service.

7.5.3 Frequencies for the Safety of Life and Property

... (5) The frequency 40.5 MHz is designated as the military joint common frequency. Use of this channel is limited to communications necessary to establish contact when other channel information is not available and for emergency communications. This frequency also may be used for search and rescue communications.

(6) The provisions of this Manual do not prevent mobile stations, or mobile earth stations, in distress from using any frequency at its disposal to attract attention, make known its position, and obtain help. (See ITU Radio Regulation Ap. 13 Part A1, § 6,1.)

7.5.4 Frequencies for Coordinating Search and Rescue Operations

... (2) The frequency 123.1 MHz, using class A3E emission, may be used by stations of the aeronautical mobile service and by other mobile and land stations engaged in coordinated search and rescue operations.

(3) The frequency 156.3 MHz [VHF Marine channel 6] may be used for communications between ship stations and aircraft stations, using G3E emission, engaged in coordinated search and rescue (SAR) operations. When control of the scene of a SAR incident is under a Coast Guard coast station, 156.3 MHz may be used by ship stations to communicate with that coast station.

Does the NIFOG authorize me to use certain frequencies?

No, the NIFOG does not grant authority to operate on any radio frequencies. Such authority can come only from the FCC or the NTIA.

Is the NIFOG the national emergency communications plan?

The NIFOG is the national guide for possible use in a situation where no other radio interoperability arrangement was promulgated by local authorities, or where emergency responders are unaware of such an arrangement. The NIFOG does NOT supersede any federal, state, tribal, territorial, local, or regional emergency communications plan. If you are dispatched to a disaster or incident scene and have no other information on how to make contact with other emergency responders, the NIFOG provides useful suggestions for which frequencies to use to attempt initial contact.

Are the interoperability channels discussed in the NIFOG available nationwide?

No, not all frequencies are available nationwide for use as described in the NIFOG. In particular, the "Non-Federal VHF Inland Interoperability Channels" may be used only in certain inland parts of the country, away from coastal areas and major waterways (see the map titled *Counties Where VTAC17/ VTAC17D May Be Used* on pages 33-34 for further details). Other channels in this plan may not be usable due to the potential for adjacent channel interference in some areas, or due to authorized on-channel uses that are different than the common uses described in the NIFOG. Use of the VCALL/ VTAC and UCALL/UTAC channels by mobiles (vehicular-mounted and handhelds) North of Line A / East of Line C is limited to 3 watts Effective Radiated Power (ERP). Any use of these frequencies above 3 watts ERP in the coordination zones, requires coordination with Canada, in accordance with the "Above 30 MHz Agreement." See FCC Public Notice DA 09-1064, release May 13, 2009.

What do I do if I experience interference to my interoperable channels?

Emergency communications on non-federal frequencies are regulated by the Federal Communications Commission (FCC). FCC rules are intended to ensure rapid, efficient communications for the purpose of promoting the safety of life and property. Rules provide authority for transmission and equipment authorization for various radio services including Maritime Services, Aviation Services and Private Land Mobile Services, e.g., public safety or emergency communications, as well as affording protection to ensure communications are effective. When federal or non-federal public safety entities experience interference, operators may request assistance from the FCC, which may include an on-scene investigation of the interference.

Notify the Statewide Interoperability Coordinator (SWIC) of any interference and conflicts.

Abridged information on interference management can be found within the NIFOG on pages 118-121.

Agencies may submit a request to the FCC 24/7 Operations Center by completing a web-based Public Safety Interference Complaint Form at the Public Safety PSIX link. Contact information is listed below.

Authority	Contact Information
FCC 24/7 Operations Center	fcc.gov/general/public-safety-support-center Public Safety Interference Complaint Form: fccprod.servicenowservices.com/psix-esix?id=psix_form (202) 418-1122 FCCOPS@fcc.gov

United States/Canada Frequency Coordination Lines

Lines A and C are intended to minimize frequency confliction between countries. Line A spans from the Pacific Ocean in Washington State to the Atlantic Ocean in Maine along the border between the United States and Canada. The exact position of the line with respect to the border varies, however in most places it is about 75 miles/ 120 km from the border (Line B is the corresponding line on the Canadian side of the Border). Line C exists in Alaska and a complementary Line D exists in Canada along the border between the United States and Canada. Due to sparse population, Line C issues occur less frequently. These coordination lines are defined in FCC Rule §1.928(e).

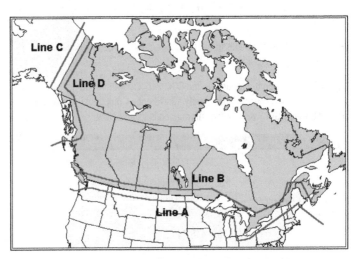

Figure 1: United States/Canada Frequency Coordination Lines

Who do I contact to use interoperability channels?

These channels can be used where licensed or authorized by FCC or NTIA, including authorization by a STA.

Plans for how these channels will be used may be in the Statewide Communications Interoperability Plan (SCIP) or the Tactical Interoperable Communications Plan (TICP) for the area of operations. Information on using 700 and 800 MHz interoperability channels may be found in the plans of your 700 MHz Regional Planning Committee or 800 MHz Regional Planning Committee. Contact your Statewide Interoperability Coordinator (SWIC) for these plans, and for additional guidance on use of these channels.

Directory of Statewide Interoperability Coordinators (SWICs):

- cisa.gov/safecom/ncswic-membership.

Directory of 700 MHz Regional Planning Committees:

- fcc.gov/general/700-mhz-rpc-directory-0

Directory of 800 MHz Regional Planning Committees:

- fcc.gov/general/800-mhz-rpc-directory

Public Safety Support Center:

- fcc.gov/general/public-safety-support-center

Applying for an STA:

- fcc.gov/applying-special-temporary-authority

How do I request a Special Temporary Authorization (STA)?

First Responders and Public Safety Entities with general FCC STA inquiries:

ULS Support at fcc.gov/available-support-services or 1-877-480-3201

During Normal FCC Business Hours:
(Monday through Friday, 8:00am - 4:30pm EST/EDT)

Tracy Simmons - STA Licensing (Part 90--Land Mobile and Public Safety), Public Safety & Homeland Security Bureau –

     phone: 717-338-2657   email: Tracy.Simmons@fcc.gov

Or file electronically:

     FCC Form 601 - ULS fcc.gov/universal-licensing-system
     Then click on Online Filing "**LOG IN**"

Outside of Normal FCC Business Hours:
(4:30pm - 8am EST/EDT, weekends, and holidays):

FCC Operations Center (FCCOC):
     phone: 202-418-1122   email: FCCOPS@fcc.gov

Federal Government Entities with general NTIA STA Requests:

U.S. Government radio stations request temporary assignment or STAs via their agency representative to the Frequency Assignment Subcommittee (FAS) of the Interdepartment Radio Advisory Committee (IRAC). See NTIA Manual section 8.3.32.

The telephone number for the NTIA Frequency Assignment Branch is: 202-482-1132.

Does the NIFOG specify exactly how to program channels?

No, there is no one-size-fits-all solution due to differing radio designs. The NIFOG uses the ANSI "Standard Channel Nomenclature for the Public Safety Interoperability Channels," APCO/NPSTC 1.104.2-2017, for channel names - see "NPSTC" on page 1.

For some channels, the standard nomenclature specifies a "direct" ("talk-around") channel for repeaters which takes an additional memory slot. Some radios have a switch for talk-around on a repeater channel and using this feature saves memory slots. Similarly, some radios may have a switch or button to enable or disable receive CTCSS; if not, another channel may be programmed so both modes are available.

Consider appropriately programming additional VHF Marine channels as possible interoperability channels (for use when properly authorized), based on local or regional use. In particular, channels used by drawbridge tenders may be appropriate; see wireless.fcc.gov/marine/vhfchanl.pdf for authorized channel uses and navcen.uscg.gov/?pageName=mtVhf for frequencies. These frequencies may be programmed only into radios certificated for Part 80 operations, and only by a person holding a First or Second Class Radiotelegraph Operator's Certificate, Radiotelegraph Operator License, or General Radiotelephone Operator License.

Recommended modes for using Federal Interoperability Channels: use analog for all Incident Response channels (CTCSS 167.9 Hz) and Law Enforcement channels LE A, LE 1, LE B, LE 10, and LE 16 (CTCSS 167.9 Hz); use P25 digital for the remaining LE channels, NAC $68F ($1679_{10}$). CTCSS should always be transmitted on the analog channels, but carrier squelch (CSQ, no CTCSS) should be used on receive. Consider allowing the user to enable or disable CTCSS on receive by a switch or button; otherwise use CSQ on receive.

How do emergency responders use the calling channels?

As you approach an incident scene or staging area, you might establish contact on a dispatch or working channel. If you can't make contact, or if no channel was designated for this purpose, attempt to make contact on one of the designated interoperability calling channels. If it is a repeater channel and you get no response, try the "direct" or "talk-around" mode if your radio has that capability. In some cases, the talk-around channel exists as a distinct channel on the radio. For example, the VHF Incident Response Federal Interoperability Channel is known as "NC 1". The talk-around for this repeater channel is known as "IR 5".

The non-federal national interoperability calling channels are VCALL10, UCALL40, 7CALL50, 7CALL70, and 8CALL90; the Federal IR and LE calling channels are "NC 1" (direct: "IR5"), "NC 2" (direct: "IR15"), "LE A", and "LE B". You may be able to learn what you need without transmitting, by just listening to radio traffic on one of these channels.

May the Nationwide Interoperability Channels be used for tests and exercises?

FCC rule §90.417 authorizes communications "in connection with mutual activities," which includes tests and exercises. FCC rule §90.411 authorizes communications for civil defense (emergency management) activities during an actual or simulated emergency, including drills and tests.

How do Search and Rescue personnel on land, on watercraft, and on aircraft coordinate by radio?

Certain VHF Marine channels are designated in this plan for Search and Rescue (SAR) interoperability. Searchers on land, in boats, and in aircraft need to be able to communicate with each other to coordinate rescues. There is no VHF channel authorized and readily available to all three communities. Some aircraft involved in SAR have VHF Marine radios, as do most boaters; but the VHF radios that many ground SAR groups use are not approved for use on maritime frequencies, and they may be incapable of being programmed to operate in the wideband FM mode used on maritime frequencies. VHF marine radios may not be used on land unless they are licensed as marine utility stations, public or private coast stations, or maritime support stations. VHF Marine channels may not be used for terrestrial search and rescue operations – they are in this plan due to the likelihood of boats being involved in SAR in coastal areas.

Frequency 155.1600 MHz is licensed to many SAR organizations. It is the *de facto* SAR interoperability channel and has been given the standardized channel name of VSAR16. We encourage public safety entities to obtain licenses for this frequency to facilitate interoperability. This is not a national interoperability frequency identified in FCC Rule §90.20(i) and must be licensed.

State or local government vehicles used to tow vessels involved in search and rescue operations are authorized to operate on maritime mobile frequencies as associated ship units. Such operations may use Distress, Safety and Calling, Intership Safety, Liaison, U.S. Coast Guard, or Maritime Control VHF intership frequencies; and may have a transmitter power of 25 watts. [FCC rule §80.115(b)] Federal vehicles have similar authorization. [NTIA Manual 8.2.29(6)(c)(6)]

Should Fire/EMS radios have the Law Enforcement interoperability channels programmed, and vice versa?

Yes, radios for public safety personnel should have as many of these interoperability channels programmed as possible, as permitted by the applicable regulations. Interoperability may require crossing jurisdictional and functional lines. On the federal interoperability channels, "Incident Response" (IR) means everybody – fire, rescue, EMS, public works, law enforcement, etc. The "law enforcement" (LE) channels will be used "primarily" for Law Enforcement activities but could be designated for other incident support if that would not hamper law enforcement activities, and if assigned by the agency in control of the incident. In practice, ESF-13 primarily uses LE-7 as the standard Federal LE interop channel between LE units.

How can I get answers to questions about the "National Interoperability Field Operations Guide", or how can I offer suggestions to improve it?

Please send your questions or comments to the Cybersecurity and Infrastructure Security Agency, at NIFOG@cisa.dhs.gov and include your name, agency or organization affiliation, and your email address.

How do I get copies of the NIFOG?

The latest version of the NIFOG can be downloaded or ordered from cisa.gov/publication/fog-documents

Regulations and Guidelines for National Interoperability

1. The FCC and NTIA rules allow for some flexibility in frequency use by personnel directly involved in a situation where there is imminent danger to human life or property. This does NOT mean "In an emergency, anything goes."

2. For communications not covered by #1, your use of a radio frequency must be authorized by:
   a. Your (or your agency's) FCC license or NTIA authorization
   b. "License by rule"– a provision in FCC rules that authorizes use of a radio frequency under specified conditions without a specific license or authorization issued to the user
   c. A "Special Temporary Authorization" provided by FCC or NTIA

3. Digital P25 operations on non-federal interoperability channels should transmit the default Network Access Code (NAC) $293 ($659_{10}$), and receive with NAC $F7E ($3966_{10}$) (accept any incoming NAC). Utilize normal squelch in programming which will use the default talkgroup - $0001($1_{10}$).

4. Default modes for using Federal Interoperability Channels: use analog for all Incident Response channels and Law Enforcement channels LE A, LE 1, LE B, LE 10, and LE 16; use P25 Digital for the remaining LE channels, NAC $68F ($1679_{10}$).

Conditions for Use of Federal Interoperability Channels

§90.25 Non-Federal use of the Federal interoperability channels.

The Commission may authorize non-Federal licensees to operate mobile and portable radio units on the frequencies listed..., provided the applicant includes with its application to the Commission, written concurrence from the Statewide Interoperability Coordinator (SWIC) or state appointed official stating that the application conforms to the agreement with a federal agency with a valid assignment from the National Telecommunications and Information Administration.

1. A non-federal entity may apply for a license, with written concurrence from the SWIC or state appointed official, which authorizes mobile and portable units to operate statewide on the Federal Interoperability Channels – See 47 CFR §90.25. Upon grant of the application, local and tribal agencies may operate under the state agency's call sign pursuant to 47 CFR §90.421.

2. The "VHF Incident Response (IR) Federal Interoperability Channel Plan", the "UHF Incident Response (IR) Federal Interoperability Channel Plan", the "VHF Law Enforcement (LE) Federal Interoperability Channel Plan", and the "UHF Law Enforcement (LE) Federal Interoperability Channel Plan" show frequencies available for use by all Federal agencies to satisfy law enforcement and public safety incident response interoperability requirements. These frequencies will be referred to hereinafter as "Federal Interoperability Channels". [NTIA Manual 4.3.16 (1)]

3. The Federal Interoperability Channels are available for use among federal agencies and between federal agencies and non-federal entities with which federal agencies have a requirement to operate. [NTIA Manual 4.3.16 (2)]

4. The channels are available to non-federal entities to enable joint federal/non-federal operations for law enforcement and incident response, subject to the condition that harmful interference will not be caused to

federal stations. These channels are restricted to interoperability communications and are not authorized for routine or administrative uses. [NTIA Manual 4.3.16 (4)]

5. Extended operations and congestion may lead to frequency conflicts. Coordination with NTIA is required to resolve these conflicts. [NTIA Manual 4.3.16 (8)]

6. Only narrowband emissions are to be used on the Federal Interoperability Channels. [NTIA Manual 4.3.16 (9)]

7. The channels listed in this document do not authorize the provisioning or use of the frequencies in any permanent infrastructure.

8. Equipment used (transmitters and receivers) must meet the standards established in Section 5.3.5.2 of the NTIA Manual:

   a. TIA/EIA 603-B for narrowband analog;

   b. TIA TSB 102.CAAB-A for narrowband digital

9. Use of these frequencies within 75 miles of the Canadian border and 5 miles of the Mexican border require special coordination and, in some cases, will not be available for use.

Federal Law Enforcement Plans

1. Channels LE-A (167.0875 MHz) and LE-B (414.0375 MHz) are designated as National Calling Channels for initial contact and will be identified in the radio as indicated in the Law Enforcement Federal Interoperability Channel Plans.

2. Initial contact communications will be established using analog FM emission (11K0F3E).

3. The interoperability channels will be identified in mobile and portable radios as indicated in the Law Enforcement Federal Interoperability Channel Plans with Continuous Tone-Controlled Squelch Systems (CTCSS) frequency 167.9 Hz and/or Network Access Code (NAC) $68F ($1679_{10}$).

Federal Incident Response Plans

1. Channels NC-1 (169.5375 MHz paired with 164.7125 MHz) and NC-2 (410.2375 MHz paired with 419.2375 MHz) are designated as the calling channels for initial contact and will be identified in the radio as indicated in the Incident Response Federal Interoperability Channel Plans.

2. Initial contact will be established using analog FM emission (11K0F3E).

3. To ensure access by stations from outside the normal area of operation, Continuous Tone-Controlled Squelch Systems (CTCSS) will not be used on the calling channels.

4. The interoperability channels will be identified in mobile and portable radios as indicated in the "VHF Incident Response (IR) Federal Interoperability Channel Plan" and the "UHF Incident Response (IR) Federal Interoperability Channel Plan."

Recommendations for Programming the Federal Interoperability Channels

1. If there is enough room in your radio, program all channels as analog and again as digital channels. If not, program as follows:

   a. Incident Response channels – all narrowband analog FM.

   b. Law Enforcement channels – program all as P25 digital with NAC $68F ($1679_{10}$) except LE A, LE 1, LE B, LE10, and LE 16 which are to be programmed analog with Tx CTCSS 167.9 Hz and no Rx CTCSS (carrier squelch, CSQ).

2. If your radio has a user-selectable option to enable/disable CTCSS on receive, you may choose to configure this option so that the user can enable the same CTCSS tone used on transmit for receive. The default configuration should be CSQ receive.

Note on using the Federal Interoperability Channels: These channels may not be used for state/state, state/local, or local/local interoperability. A federal entity must be involved when used.

INTEROPERABILITY CHANNELS

Conventions of Use for Interoperability

Plain Language and Common Terminology

10-Codes and other coded language lack common universality to be of benefit in multi-agency, multi discipline incidents. It is important that responders and incident managers use plain language and common terminology. There simply is little or no room for misunderstanding in an emergency situation.

The use of plain language in emergency response is matter of public safety, especially the safety of first responders and those affected by the incident. It is critical that all local responders, as well as those coming into the impacted area from other jurisdictions and other states as well as the federal government, know and utilize commonly established operational structures, terminology, policies and procedures.

The use of common terminology is about the ability of area commanders, State and local EOC personnel, federal operational coordinators, and emergency responders to communicate clearly with each other and effectively coordinate response activities, no matter what the size, scope or complexity of the incident. The ability of responders from different jurisdictions and different disciplines to work together depends greatly on their ability to communicate with each other.

Interoperability Communications Order Model

Communications Order Model refers to the order of the radio identification or callsign of the sender and receiver is spoken. The prevailing model in the U.S. has a common order in how a message is initiated. Often, this model is referred to a "Hey you, It's me." The sender states the unit/person called, followed by the sender's unit or name.

Example: "Dispatch, this is Engine 21." The response is the reverse: "Engine 21, this is Dispatch, go ahead."

Establishing this order model increases interoperability so that units are aware which identification/callsign comes first. This model is used by the amateur radio community, the Department of Defense, the US Coast Guard, the National Guard, many public safety agencies across the country, and is endorsed by APCO and SAFECOM.

Interoperability "Watch-Out" Situations

o   Incidents using channels in more than one radio frequency band.

o   Same channel/frequency being used with a local name outside of the ANSI standard.

o   Unable to communicate critical information due to radio congestion.

o   Unfamiliar with radio system (s) or assigned radio functionality.

o   Instructions and assignments not clear.

o   Have no or inadequate communication with responders or supervisors.

o   Dispatch to Dispatch channel patching.

o   Inadequate number of tactical channels available or assigned.

o   Multiple conversations on the same talkgroup or channel.

o   Radio systems used for interoperability do not completely support the incident and lack good radio coverage.

o   High levels of background noise.

o   Emergency button activation – Who is receiving the notification, does it work the same for all radios?

o   Multiple agencies performing radio programming at the incident.

o   Organizations in the system do not use the same vocabulary.

o   Mobile gateway devices being used in a strategic (wide-area) rather than tactical (local) environment.

o   Multiple mobile gateways available at the incident.

o   Ensure the activation and deactivation of gateway patches are properly announced.

o   When a single COML for the incident has not been identified.

o   Working in the deep interior of a building, tunnel, or area below grade or above grade.

ICS 205 Sample & Channel Instructions

INCIDENT RADIO COMMUNICATIONS PLAN		Incident Name	Twine Ball IC		Date/Time Prepared	7/26/2021 1045		Operational Period Date/Time	7/27/2021 0700 - 7/28/2021 0700	

Ch #	Function	Channel Name/Trunked Radio System Talkgroup	Assignment	RX Freq	RX Tone / NAC	TX Freq	TX Tone / NAC	Mode A, D, M	Remarks
1	Tactical	VSAR16	SAR	155.1600	127.3	155.1600	127.3	A	Gateway Patch 1
2	Tactical	IR 12	SAR	410.8375	CSQ	419.8374	167.9	A	Gateway Patch 1
3	Tactical	UTAC43	SAR	453.8625	156.7	458.8625	156.7	A	Gateway Patch 1
4	Tactical	8TAC94	SAR	853.0125	156.7	808.0125	156.7	A	Gateway Patch 1
5	Tactical	VTAC11	DIV. A	151.1375	156.7	151.1375	156.7	A	
6	Tactical	CC TAC 3	DIV. B	151.4150	DPL 032	151.4150	DPL 032	A	
7	Tactical	VTAC14	DIV. C	159.4725	156.7	159.4725	156.7	A	
8	Tactical	CNTL CTY TRUNK	DIV. D	Talkgroup 21		Talkgroup 21		D	
9	Tactical	CNTL CTY TRUNK	DIV. E	Talkgroup 55		Talkgroup 55		D	
10	Tactical	VMED28	Medical	155.3400	CSQ	155.3400	156.7	A	
11	Tactical	VFIRE23	Fire	154.2950	CSQ	154.2950	88.5	A	
12	Tactical	CC JACKSON	LE	153.8600	CSQ	155.8800	100.0	A	
13	Command	7GTAC77	COMMAND	774.85625	$F7E	804.85625	$293	D	Gateway Patch 2
14	Command	CNTL CTY TRUNK	COMMAND	Talkgroup 14		Talkgroup 14		D	Gateway Patch 2
15									
16									

Prepared By (Communications Unit)	Incident Location	
Darwin Cawker, COML 303-499-7111	Central City	39-30-33.2 N, 99-26-01.3 W

The convention calls for frequency lists to show four digits after the decimal place. Mode refers to either "A" or "D" indicating analog or digital (e.g. Project 25) or "M" indicating mixed mode. All channels are shown as if programmed in a control station, mobile or portable radio. Repeater and base stations must be programmed with the Rx and Tx reversed. Ensure activation and deactivation of gateway patches are properly announced. Personnel using patched channels or talkgroups should use agency-specific unit identification, plain language, and common terminology.

ICS 205   3/2007

25

Column Title	Instructions
Function	Enter the Net function each channel or talkgroup will be used for (e.g. Command, Tactical, Air - to-Ground, Support, Staging).
Channel Name/Trunked Radio System Talkgroup	Enter the nomenclature or commonly used name for the channel or talk group.
Assignment	Enter the name of the ICS Branch/Division/Group/Section to which this channel/talkgroup will be assigned.
RX (Receive) Frequency	Enter the Receive Frequency (RX Freq) as the mobile or portable subscriber would be programmed using xxx.xxxx out to four decimal places
RX Tone/NAC	Enter the Receive Continuous Tone Coded Squelch System (CTCSS) subaudible tone (RX Tone) or Network Access Code (RX NAC) for the receive frequency as the mobile or portable subscriber would be programmed.
TX (Transmit) Frequency	Enter the Transmit Frequency (TX Freq) as the mobile or portable subscriber would be programmed using xxx.xxxx out to four decimal places
TX Tone/NAC	Enter the Transmit Continuous Tone Coded Squelch System (CTCSS) subaudible tone (TX Tone) or Network Access Code (TX NAC) for the transmit frequency as the mobile or portable subscriber would be programmed.
Mode (A, D, or M)	Enter "A" for analog operation, "D" for digital operation, or "M" for mixed mode operation.
Remarks	Enter miscellaneous information concerning repeater locations, information concerning patched channels or talkgroups using links or gateways, etc.
Special Instructions	Enter any special instructions (e.g., using cross-band repeaters, encryption, etc.) or other emergency communications needs).

Notes on Interoperability Channels

Interoperability channels exist in many forms. There are channels that are national, federal, regional, and local. They all have different rules and conventions for use. Some require licensing, and/or a memorandum of agreement/understanding (MOA/MOU) or letter of authorization (LOA), and some do not. Coordination is key for all interoperability channels. Inclusion of frequencies in the NIFOG does not convey authority to operate.

Field Programming

Caution should be used when programming in the field. Transposition of a single digit can render a channel unusable. Pre-programing, verification and testing are recommended. Cloning of preprogramed channels is preferred over field programming.

- All frequencies in this guide represent mobile and portable programming.
- Radio frequencies are shown in Megahertz (MHz) unless otherwise noted.
- CTCSS tone frequencies are in Hertz (Hz).
- Frequencies above 138 MHz are narrowband FM, unless otherwise noted.
- Direct (Simplex) mode: receive & transmit on "Mobile RX" freq.; add "D" to channel name (Except in VHF as indicated).
- Repeater mode: mobile transmits on "Mobile TX" freq., receives on "Base & Mobile TX" freq.
- Use of a tactical repeater with these channels must be licensed or authorized by STA. (FCC Station Class FB2T).
- For programming P25 LMR Equipment, "$" indicates hexadecimal value, "10" subscript indicates decimal value.

VHF National Interoperability Channels
Low Band – LLAW & LFIRE

Assignment	Channel Name	Mobile RX Freq. (MHz)	Mobile RX CTCSS/NAC	Mobile TX Freq. (MHz)	Mobile TX CTCSS/NAC
Law Enforcement	LLAW1	39.4600	156.7	45.8600	156.7
Law Enforcement	LLAW1D	39.4600	156.7	39.4600	156.7
Fire*	LFIRE2	39.4800	156.7	45.8800	156.7
Fire*	LFIRE2D	39.4800	156.7	39.4800	156.7
Law Enforcement	LLAW3	45.8600	156.7	39.4600	156.7
Law Enforcement	LLAW3D	45.8600	156.7	45.8600	156.7
Fire*	LFIRE4	45.8800	156.7	39.4800	156.7
Fire	LFIRE4D	45.8800	156.7	45.8800	156.7

* Proposed for use. Frequency 39.4800 MHz is pending FCC assignment for exclusive fire intersystem use.

- Use emission – 16K0F3E (5 kHz deviation wideband Analog FM)

VHF National Interoperability Channels
VHF Tactical Simplex – VCALL & VTAC

CAUTION: Ensure coordination between VTAC simplex and repeater operations. These frequencies are used to create utilizing the tactical repeater channels listed for VTAC33-38.

Assignment	Channel Name	Mobile RX Freq. (MHz)	Mobile RX CTCSS/NAC	Mobile TX Freq. (MHz)	Mobile TX CTCSS/NAC
Calling	VCALL10	155.7525	156.7	155.7525	156.7
Tactical *	VTAC11	151.1375	156.7	151.1375	156.7
Tactical *	VTAC12	154.4525	156.7	154.4525	156.7
Tactical	VTAC13	158.7375	156.7	158.7375	156.7
Tactical	VTAC14	159.4725	156.7	159.4725	156.7

- Authorized emission – 11K0F3E (2.5 kHz deviation narrowband Analog FM) – 47 CFR §90.20(d)(80)
- Encryption may not be used – 47 CFR §90.20(i)
- Limited to 3 watts ERP North of Line A or East of Line C.
*VTAC11-12 may not be used in Puerto Rico or the US Virgin Islands.
- VCALL10, VTAC11-14 utilize a 156.7 Hz CTCSS Mobile TX tone which differs from the VTAC33-38 Tactical Repeater Channels which utilize a 136.5 Hz CTCSS Mobile TX tone.

VHF National Interoperability Channels
VHF Tactical Repeater - VTAC

CAUTION: Ensure coordination between VTAC simplex and repeater operations. These channels are created by utilizing the frequencies listed for VTAC11-14.

Assignment	Channel Name	Mobile RX Freq. (MHz)	Mobile RX CTCSS/NAC	Mobile TX Freq. (MHz)	Mobile TX CTCSS/NAC
Tactical Repeater *	VTAC33	159.4725	156.7	151.1375	136.5
Tactical Repeater *	VTAC34	158.7375	156.7	154.4525	136.5
Tactical Repeater	VTAC35	159.4725	156.7	158.7375	136.5
Tactical Repeater * •	VTAC36	151.1375	156.7	159.4725	136.5
Tactical Repeater * •	VTAC37	154.4525	156.7	158.7375	136.5
Tactical Repeater •	VTAC38	158.7375	156.7	159.4725	136.5

- Authorized emission – 11K0F3E (2.5 kHz deviation narrowband Analog FM) – 47 CFR §90.20(d)(80)
- Encryption may not be used – 47 CFR §90.20(i)
- Limited to 3 watts ERP North of Line A or East of Line C.
- VTAC33-38 utilize a 136.5 Hz CTCSS Mobile TX tone which differs from the VTAC11-14 Simplex Channels which utilize a 156.7 Hz CTCSS Mobile TX tone.
- VTAC33-35 are the reverse of VTAC36-38 to allow for mitigation of any potential co-site interference.
* VTAC33-34, and VTAC36-37 may not be used in Puerto Rico or the US Virgin Islands.
• VTAC36-38 are preferred; VTAC33-35 should be used only when necessary due to interference.

VHF National Interoperability Channels
VHF Inland – VTAC17

LICENSING REQUIRED: These frequencies are NOT covered by the "Blanket Authorization" for nationwide interoperability channels. Use of these channels must be licensed or authorized by STA.

Assignment	Channel Name	Mobile RX Freq. (MHz)	Mobile RX CTCSS/NAC	Mobile TX Freq. (MHz)	Mobile TX CTCSS/NAC
Tactical	VTAC17	161.8500	156.7	157.2500	156.7
Tactical	VTAC17D	161.8500	156.7	161.8500	156.7

For VTAC17/VTAC17D only: Base stations: 50 watts max, antenna HAAT 400 feet max. Mobile stations: 20 watts max, antenna HAAT 15 feet max. These channels are for tactical use and may not be operated on board aircraft in flight. These channels use 2.5 kHz deviation narrowband Analog FM and are available only in certain inland areas at least 100 miles from a major waterway. These channels use the same frequencies as VHF Marine channel 25, which uses 5 kHz deviation wideband Analog FM. Use only where authorized. See map on next page. In these authorized areas, interoperability communications have priority over grandfathered public coast and public safety licensees. See 47 CFR §90.20(g)(3).

- Authorized emission – 11K0F3E (2.5 kHz deviation narrowband analog FM)
- Limited to 3 watts ERP North of Line A or East of Line C.

Counties Where VTAC17/VTAC17D May Be Used

Numbers Indicate VHF Public Coast Station Areas – see 47CFR 80.371(c)(ii)

CA: Alpine, Inyo, Lassen, Mono, Plumas, Sierra

KS: Cheyenne, Gove, Logan, Sheridan, Sherman, Thomas, Wallace

MN: Kittson, Lake of the Woods, Marshall, Pennington, Polk, Red Lake, Roseau

NE: Arthur, Banner, Blaine, Box Butte, Chase, Cherry, Cheyenne, Dawes, Deuel, Dundy, Garden, Grant, Hooker, Keith, Kimball, Lincoln, Logan, McPherson, Morrill, Perkins, Scotts Bluff, Sheridan, Sioux, Thomas

OK: Beckham, Custer, Dewey, Ellis, Greer, Harmon, Harper, Jackson, Kiowa, Roger Mills, Washita, Woodward

---

All of CO, MT, NM, NV, UT, & WY

All counties in AZ ID & ND except: **AZ:** La Paz, Yuma

ID: Benewah, Bonner, Boundary, Clearwater, Idaho, Kootenai, Latah, Lewis, Nez Perce, & Shoshone

ND: Barnes, Cass, Dickey, Foster, Griggs, LaMoure, Pierce, Ransom, Richland, Sargent, Sheridan, Stutsman, Wells

OR: Harney, Malheur

SD: All counties except Aurora, Beadle, Bon Homme, Brookings, Brule, Buffalo, Charles Mix, Clark, Clay, Codington, Davison, Deuel, Douglas, Grant, Gregory, Hamlin, Hand, Hanson, Hughes, Hutchinson, Hyde, Jerauld, Kingsbury, Lake, Lincoln, Lyman, McCook, Miner, Minnehaha, Moody, Roberts, Sanborn, Stanley, Sully, Tripp, Turner, Union, Yankton

TX Counties – see page 34

Texas Counties Where VTAC17/VTAC17D May Be Used
(see page 33)

Andrews	Dawson	Hudspeth	Moore	Swisher
Armstrong	Deaf Smith	Hutchinson	Motley	Taylor
Bailey	Dickens	Irion	Nolan	Terrell
Borden	Donley	Jeff Davis	Ochiltree	Terry
Brewster	Ector	Jones	Oldham	Tom Green
Briscoe	Edwards	Kent	Parmer	Upton
Callahan	El Paso	Kimble	Pecos	Val Verde
Carson	Fisher	King	Potter	Ward
Castro	Floyd	Kinney	Presidio	Wheeler
Childress	Gaines	Knox	Randall	Winkler
Cochran	Garza	Lamb	Reagan	Yoakum
Coke	Glasscock	Lipscomb	Reeves	
Collingsworth	Gray	Loving	Roberts	
Concho	Hale	Lubbock	Runnels	
Cottle	Hall	Lynn	Schleicher	
Crane	Hansford	McCulloch	Scurry	
Crockett	Hartley	Martin	Sherman	
Crosby	Haskell	Menard	Sterling	
Culberson	Hockley	Midland	Stonewell	
Dallam	Howard	Mitchell	Sutton	

LICENSING REQUIRED: These frequencies are NOT covered by the "Blanket Authorization" for nationwide interoperability channels. Use of these channels must be licensed or authorized by STA. Availability subject to other licensed users in the same area.

Assignment	Channel Name	Mobile RX Freq. (MHz)	Mobile RX CTCSS/NAC	Mobile TX Freq. (MHz)	Mobile TX CTCSS/NAC
SAR Common*	VSAR16	155.1600	127.3	155.1600	127.3
Fire Mutual Aid (Not available in Puerto Rico and the U.S Virgin Islands)	VFIRE21	154.2800		154.2800	
	VFIRE22	154.2650		154.2650	
	VFIRE23	154.2950		154.2950	
	VFIRE24	154.2725		154.2725	
	VFIRE25	154.2875		154.2875	
	VFIRE26	154.3025		154.3025	
EMS Mutual Aid	VMED28	155.3400	CSQ	155.3400	156.7
	VMED29	155.3475		155.3475	
Law Enforcement Mutual Aid	VLAW31	155.4750		155.4750	
	VLAW32	155.4825		155.4825	

CTCSS tones vary by jurisdiction. Rules for use of these channels are contained in 47 CFR 90.20. EXCEPT for VSAR16, the recommended CTCSS tones are 156.7 receive and transmit for all channels on this page for interoperability; local use may specify other tones.

VHF Incident Response (IR) Federal Interoperability Channels

LICENSING REQUIRED: These frequencies are **NOT** covered by the blanket authorization for nationwide interoperability channels. For Interoperability with Federal Stations Only.

Suggested Assignment	Channel Name	Mobile RX Freq. (MHz)	Mobile RX CTCSS/NAC	Mobile TX Freq. (MHz)	Mobile TX CTCSS/NAC
Incident Calling	NC 1	169.5375	CSQ	164.7125	167.9
Incident Command	IR 1	170.0125	CSQ	165.2500	167.9
Medical Evacuation (Direct)	IR 2	170.4125	CSQ	165.9625	167.9
Logistics Control	IR 3	170.6875	CSQ	166.5750	167.9
Interagency Convoy	IR 4	173.0375	CSQ	167.3250	167.9
Incident Calling (Direct)	IR 5	169.5375	CSQ	169.5375	167.9
Incident Command (Direct)	IR 6	170.0125	CSQ	170.0125	167.9
Medical Evacuation	IR 7	170.4125	CSQ	170.4125	167.9
Logistics Control (Direct)	IR 8	170.6875	CSQ	170.6875	167.9
Interagency Convoy (Direct)	IR 9	173.0375	CSQ	173.0375	167.9

See "Conditions for Use of Federal Interoperability Channels" on pages 19-22.

Default operation should be carrier squelch receive; CTCSS 167.9 transmit. If the user can enable/disable CTCSS without reprogramming the radio, the indicated CTCSS tone also could be programmed for receive, and the user instructed how and when to enable/disable.

VHF Law Enforcement (LE) Federal Interoperability Channels

LICENSING REQUIRED: These frequencies are **NOT** covered by the blanket authorization for nationwide interoperability channels. For Interoperability with Federal Stations Only.

Suggested Assignment	Channel Name	Mobile RX Freq. (MHz)	Mobile RX CTCSS/NAC	Mobile TX Freq. (MHz)	Mobile TX CTCSS/NAC
Calling (Analog)	LE A	167.0875	CSQ	167.0875	167.9
Tactical (Analog)	LE 1	167.0875	CSQ	162.0875	167.9
Tactical	LE 2	167.2500	$68F	162.2625	$68F
Tactical	LE 3	167.7500	$68F	162.8375	$68F
Tactical	LE 4	168.1125	$68F	163.2875	$68F
Tactical	LE 5	168.4625	$68F	163.4250	$68F
Tactical (Direct for LE 2)	LE 6	167.2500	$68F	167.2500	$68F
Tactical (Direct for LE 3)	LE 7	167.7500	$68F	167.7500	$68F
Tactical (Direct for LE 4)	LE 8	168.1125	$68F	168.1125	$68F
Tactical (Direct for LE 5)	LE 9	168.4625	$68F	168.4625	$68F

See "Conditions for Use of Federal Interoperability Channels" on pages 19-22.

CTCSS on receive only if user selectable; else CSQ.

"$" indicates hexadecimal value

NOAA Weather Radio (NWR) "All Hazards" Broadcasts

weather.gov/nwr/

NWR broadcasts National Weather Service (NWS) warnings, watches, forecasts, and other non-weather-related hazard information 24 hours a day. Frequencies listed below are used in the US & Canada. These channels should be programmed as analog wideband FM (16K0F3E) RECEIVE ONLY. Tone Alarm: NWS will send a 1050 Hz tone alarm before broadcasting most warnings and many watch messages. The alarm will activate all the receivers equipped to receive it, even if the audio is turned off. This is especially useful for warnings during the night.

United States & Canada - Weather Radio Broadcasts – Receive Only						
162.4000	162.4250	162.4500	162.4750	162.5000	162.5250	162.5500

NOAA Weather Radio outages or transmitter problems: Listings weather.gov/nwr/outages
Report form weather.gov/nwr/nwr_outage_report or call 1-888-886-1227 or email nwroutage@noaa.gov

Marine Weather Broadcasts - United States Coast Guard

The U.S. Coast Guard broadcasts coastal forecasts and storm warnings of interest to mariners on VHF channel 22A (157.1000 MHz) following an initial announcement on VHF channel 16 (156.8000 MHz). For broadcast times and sector listings: weather.gov/marine/uscg_broadcasts

Continuous Marine Broadcasts – Canadian Coast Guard

The Canadian Coast Guard broadcasts marine weather information, provided by Environment Canada, in certain coastal locations on the Atlantic and Pacific Coasts, as well as the coastal areas of the Great Lakes primarily on these channels:

VHF Marine Channel 21b (161.6500 MHz) and VHF Marine Channel 83b (161.7750 MHz)

UHF Nationwide Interoperability Channels
UCALL & UTAC

Assignment	Channel Name	Mobile RX Freq. (MHz)	Mobile RX CTCSS/NAC	Mobile TX Freq. (MHz)	Mobile TX CTCSS/NAC
Calling	UCALL40	453.2125	156.7	458.2125	156.7
Calling Direct	UCALL40D	453.2125	156.7	453.2125	156.7
Tactical Repeater	UTAC41	453.4625	156.7	458.4625	156.7
Tactical Direct	UTAC41D	453.4625	156.7	453.4625	156.7
Tactical Repeater	UTAC42	453.7125	156.7	458.7125	156.7
Tactical Direct	UTAC42D	453.7125	156.7	453.7125	156.7
Tactical Repeater	UTAC43	453.8625	156.7	458.8625	156.7
Tactical Direct	UTAC43D	453.8625	156.7	453.8625	156.7

- Authorized emission – 11K0F3E (2.5 kHz deviation narrowband Analog FM) – 47 CFR §90.20(d)(80)
- Encryption may not be used – 47 CFR §90.20(i)
- Limited to 3 watts ERP North of Line A or East of Line C.

UHF Incident Response (IR) Federal Interoperability Channels

LICENSING REQUIRED: These frequencies are **NOT** covered by the blanket authorization for nationwide interoperability channels. **For Interoperability with Federal Stations Only.**

Suggested Assignment	Channel Name	Mobile RX Freq. (MHz)	Mobile RX CTCSS/NAC	Mobile TX Freq. (MHz)	Mobile TX CTCSS/NAC
Incident Calling	NC 2	410.2375	CSQ	419.2375	167.9
Ad hoc Assignment	IR 10	410.4375	CSQ	419.4375	167.9
Ad hoc Assignment	IR 11	410.6375	CSQ	419.6375	167.9
SAR Incident Command	IR 12	410.8375	CSQ	419.8375	167.9
Ad hoc Assignment	IR 13	413.1875	CSQ	413.1875	167.9
Interagency Convoy	IR 14	413.2125	CSQ	413.2125	167.9
Incident Calling (Direct)	IR 15	410.2375	CSQ	410.2375	167.9
Ad hoc (Direct for IR 10)	IR 16	410.4375	CSQ	410.4375	167.9
Ad hoc (Direct for IR 11)	IR 17	410.6375	CSQ	410.6375	167.9
SAR Incident Command (Direct)	IR 18	410.8375	CSQ	410.8375	167.9

See "Conditions for Use of Federal Interoperability Channels" on pages 19-22.

Default operation should be carrier squelch receive; CTCSS 167.9 transmit. If the user can enable/disable CTCSS without reprogramming the radio, the indicated CTCSS tone also could be programmed for receive, and the user instructed how and when to enable/disable.

UHF Law Enforcement (LE) Federal Interoperability Channels

LICENSING REQUIRED: These frequencies are **NOT** covered by the blanket authorization for nationwide interoperability channels. For Interoperability with Federal Stations Only.

Suggested Assignment	Channel Name	Mobile RX Freq. (MHz)	Mobile RX CTCSS/NAC	Mobile TX Freq. (MHz)	Mobile TX CTCSS/NAC
Calling (Analog)	LE B	414.0375	CSQ	414.0375	167.9
Tactical (Analog)	LE 10	409.9875	CSQ	418.9875	167.9
Tactical	LE 11	410.1875	$68F	419.1875	$68F
Tactical	LE 12	410.6125	$68F	419.6125	$68F
Tactical	LE 13	414.0625	$68F	414.0625	$68F
Tactical	LE 14	414.3125	$68F	414.3125	$68F
Tactical	LE 15	414.3375	$68F	414.3375	$68F
Tactical (Direct for LE 10)	LE 16	409.9875	CSQ	409.9875	167.9
Tactical (Direct for LE 11)	LE 17	410.1875	$68F	410.1875	$68F
Tactical (Direct for LE 12)	LE 18	410.6125	$68F	410.6125	$68F

See "Conditions for Use of Federal Interoperability Channels" on pages 19-22.

CTCSS on receive only if user selectable; else CSQ.

"$" indicates hexadecimal value

UHF Medical (MED, EMS) Channels

LICENSING REQUIRED: These frequencies are **NOT** covered by the blanket authorization for nationwide interoperability channels. Availability subject to other licensed users in the same area.

Assignment	Channel Name	Mobile RX Freq. (MHz)	Mobile RX CTCSS/NAC	Mobile TX Freq. (MHz)	Mobile TX CTCSS/NAC
Dispatch*	MED-9	462.9500	See Notes	467.9500	See Notes
	MED-9D	462.9500	"	462.9500	"
Dispatch*	MED-92	462.9625	"	467.9625	"
	MED-92D	462.9625	"	462.9625	"
Dispatch*	MED-10	462.9750	"	467.9750	"
	MED-10D	462.9750	"	462.9750	"
Dispatch*	MED-102	462.9875	"	467.9875	"
	MED-102D	462.9875	"	462.9875	"
Medical	MED-1	463.0000	"	468.0000	"
Medical (Direct)	MED-1D	463.0000	"	463.0000	"

* Used primarily for dispatch; may be used for mutual aid. 47CFR90.20(d)(65).
Recommended CTCSS tones are 156.7 Hz receive and transmit for all channels on this page for interoperability; local use may specify other CTCSS tones as required by local plan.

UHF Medical (MED, EMS) Channels

LICENSING REQUIRED: These frequencies are **NOT** covered by the blanket authorization for nationwide interoperability channels. Availability subject to other licensed users in the same area.

Assignment	Channel Name	Mobile RX Freq. (MHz)	Mobile RX CTCSS/NAC	Mobile TX Freq. (MHz)	Mobile TX CTCSS/NAC
Medical	MED-12	463.0125	See Notes	468.0125	See Notes
Medical (Direct)	MED-12D	463.0125	"	463.0125	"
Medical	MED-2	463.0250	"	468.0250	"
Medical (Direct)	MED-2D	463.0250	"	463.0250	"
Medical	MED-22	463.0375	"	468.0375	"
Medical (Direct)	MED-22D	463.0375	"	463.0375	"
Medical	MED-3	463.0500	"	468.0500	"
Medical (Direct)	MED-3D	463.0500	"	463.0500	"
Medical	MED-32	463.0625	"	468.0625	"
Medical (Direct)	MED-32D	463.0625	"	463.0625	"

Recommended CTCSS tones are 156.7 Hz receive and transmit for all channels on this page for interoperability; local use may specify other CTCSS tones as required by local plan.

UHF Medical (MED, EMS) Channels

LICENSING REQUIRED: These frequencies are **NOT** covered by the blanket authorization for nationwide interoperability channels. Availability subject to other licensed users in the same area.

Assignment	Channel Name	Mobile RX Freq. (MHz)	Mobile RX CTCSS/NAC	Mobile TX Freq. (MHz)	Mobile TX CTCSS/NAC
Medical	MED-4	463.0750	See Notes	468.0750	See Notes
Medical (Direct)	MED-4D	463.0750	"	463.0750	"
Medical	MED-42	463.0875	"	468.0875	"
Medical (Direct)	MED-42D	463.0875	"	463.0875	"
Medical	MED-5	463.1000	"	468.1000	"
Medical (Direct)	MED-5D	463.1000	"	463.1000	"
Medical	MED-52	463.1125	"	468.1125	"
Medical (Direct)	MED-52D	463.1125	"	463.1125	"
Medical	MED-6	463.1250	"	468.1250	"
Medical (Direct)	MED-6D	463.1250	"	463.1250	"

Recommended CTCSS tones are 156.7 Hz receive and transmit for all channels on this page for interoperability; local use may specify other CTCSS tones as required by local plan.

UHF Medical (MED, EMS) Channels

LICENSING REQUIRED: These frequencies are **NOT** covered by the blanket authorization for nationwide interoperability channels. Availability subject to other licensed users in the same area.

Assignment	Channel Name	Mobile RX Freq. (MHz)	Mobile RX CTCSS/NAC	Mobile TX Freq. (MHz)	Mobile TX CTCSS/NAC
Medical	MED-62	463.1375	See Notes	468.1375	See Notes
Medical (Direct)	MED-62D	463.1375	" "	463.1375	" "
Medical	MED-7	463.1500	" "	468.1500	" "
Medical (Direct)	MED-7D	463.1500	" "	463.1500	" "
Medical	MED-72	463.1625	" "	468.1625	" "
Medical (Direct)	MED-72D	463.1625	" "	463.1625	" "
Medical	MED-8	463.1750	" "	468.1750	" "
Medical (Direct)	MED-8D	463.1750	" "	463.1750	" "
Medical	MED-82	463.1875	" "	468.1875	" "
Medical (Direct)	MED-82D	463.1875	" "	463.1875	" "

Recommended CTCSS tones are 156.7 Hz receive and transmit for all channels on this page for interoperability; local use may specify other CTCSS tones as required by local plan.

700 MHz Nationwide Interoperability Channels

| TX NAC: $293 ($659_{10}$) | RX NAC $F7E ($3966_{10}$). | | Default Talk Group ID: $0001 ($1_{10}$) |

"$" indicates hexadecimal value, "$_{10}$" subscript indicates decimal value.

Assignment	Channel Name	Mobile RX Freq. (MHz)	Mobile RX CTCSS/NAC	Mobile TX Freq. (MHz)	Mobile TX CTCSS/NAC
Calling Channel *	7CALL50	769.24375	$F7E	799.24375	$293
Calling Channel *	7CALL50D	769.24375	$F7E	769.24375	$293
General Public Safety	7TAC51	769.14375	$F7E	799.14375	$293
General Public Safety	7TAC51D	769.14375	$F7E	769.14375	$293
General Public Safety	7TAC52	769.64375	$F7E	799.64375	$293
General Public Safety	7TAC52D	769.64375	$F7E	769.64375	$293
General Public Safety	7TAC53	770.14375	$F7E	800.14375	$293
General Public Safety	7TAC53D	770.14375	$F7E	770.14375	$293
General Public Safety	7TAC54	770.64375	$F7E	800.64375	$293
General Public Safety	7TAC54D	770.64375	$F7E	770.64375	$293

- Authorized emission – 8K10F1E (Digital P25 Phase I Modulation) – 47 CFR §90.548(a)(1)
- Utilize normal squelch in programming which will use the default talkgroup - $0001 ($1_{10}$).
- AES Encryption permitted on all but the two nationwide interoperability calling channels. Must have accessible switch
  or other readily accessible control that permits the radio user to disable encryption. 47 CFR §90.553
* Recommended as PRIMARY calling channel for 700 MHz Band.

700 MHz Nationwide Interoperability Channels

Assignment	Channel Name	Mobile RX Freq. (MHz)	Mobile RX CTCSS/NAC	Mobile TX Freq. (MHz)	Mobile TX CTCSS/NAC
General Public Safety	7TAC55	769.74375	$F7E	799.74375	$293
General Public Safety	7TAC55D	769.74375	$F7E	769.74375	$293
General Public Safety	7TAC56	770.24375	$F7E	800.24375	$293
General Public Safety	7TAC56D	770.24375	$F7E	770.24375	$293
Other Public Safety	7GTAC57	770.99375	$F7E	800.99375	$293
Other Public Safety	7GTAC57D	770.99375	$F7E	770.99375	$293
Mobile Repeater	7MOB59	770.89375	$F7E	800.89375	$293
Mobile Repeater	7MOB59D	770.89375	$F7E	770.89375	$293
Law Enforcement	7LAW61	770.39375	$F7E	800.39375	$293
Law Enforcement	7LAW61D	770.39375	$F7E	770.39375	$293
Law Enforcement	7LAW62	770.49375	$F7E	800.49375	$293
Law Enforcement	7LAW62D	770.49375	$F7E	770.49375	$293

- Authorized emission – 8K10F1E (Digital P25 Phase I Modulation) – 47 CFR §90.548(a)(1)
- Utilize normal squelch in programming which will use the default talkgroup - $0001 ($1_{10}$).
- AES Encryption permitted on all but the two nationwide interoperability calling channel. Must have accessible switch or other readily accessible control that permits the radio user to disable encryption. 47 CFR §90.553

700 MHz Nationwide Interoperability Channels

Assignment	Channel Name	Mobile RX Freq. (MHz)	Mobile RX CTCSS/NAC	Mobile TX Freq. (MHz)	Mobile TX CTCSS/NAC
Fire	7FIRE63	769.89375	$F7E	799.89375	$293
Fire	7FIRE63D	769.89375	$F7E	769.89375	$293
Fire	7FIRE64	769.99375	$F7E	799.99375	$293
Fire	7FIRE64D	769.99375	$F7E	769.99375	$293
EMS	7MED65	769.39375	$F7E	799.39375	$293
EMS	7MED65D	769.39375	$F7E	769.39375	$293
EMS	7MED66	769.49375	$F7E	799.49375	$293
EMS	7MED66D	769.49375	$F7E	769.49375	$293
Mobile Data *	7DATA69	770.74375	$F7E	800.74375	$293
Mobile Data *	7DATA69D	770.74375	$F7E	770.74375	$293

- Authorized emission – 8K10F1E (Digital P25 Phase I Modulation) – 47 CFR §90.548(a)(1)
- Utilize normal squelch in programming which will use the default talkgroup - $0001 (1₁₀).
- AES Encryption permitted on all but the two nationwide interoperability calling channel. Must have accessible switch or other readily accessible control that permits the radio user to disable encryption. 47 CFR §90.553

* Voice communications are permitted on 7DATA69 / 7DATA69D on a secondary basis – 90.531(b)(1)(i).

700 MHz Nationwide Interoperability Channels

Assignment	Channel Name	Mobile RX Freq. (MHz)	Mobile RX CTCSS/NAC	Mobile TX Freq. (MHz)	Mobile TX CTCSS/NAC
Calling Channel **	7CALL70	773.25625	$F7E	803.25625	$293
Calling Channel **	7CALL70D	773.25625	$F7E	773.25625	$293
General Public Safety	7TAC71	773.10625	$F7E	803.10625	$293
General Public Safety	7TAC71D	773.10625	$F7E	773.10625	$293
General Public Safety	7TAC72	773.60625	$F7E	803.60625	$293
General Public Safety	7TAC72D	773.60625	$F7E	773.60625	$293
General Public Safety	7TAC73	774.10625	$F7E	804.10625	$293
General Public Safety	7TAC73D	774.10625	$F7E	774.10625	$293
General Public Safety	7TAC74	774.60625	$F7E	804.60625	$293
General Public Safety	7TAC74D	774.60625	$F7E	774.60625	$293

- Authorized emission – 8K10F1E (Digital P25 Phase I Modulation) – 47 CFR §90.548(a)(1)
- Utilize normal squelch in programming which will use the default talkgroup - $0001 (1$_{10}$).
- AES Encryption permitted on all but the two nationwide interoperability calling channel. Must have accessible switch or other readily accessible control that permits the radio user to disable encryption. 47 CFR §90.553
** Recommended as SECONDARY calling channel or INCIDENT calling channel for 700 MHz band.

700 MHz Nationwide Interoperability Channels

Assignment	Channel Name	Mobile RX Freq. (MHz)	Mobile RX CTCSS/NAC	Mobile TX Freq. (MHz)	Mobile TX CTCSS/NAC
General Public Safety	7TAC75	773.75625	$F7E	803.75625	$293
General Public Safety	7TAC75D	773.75625	$F7E	773.75625	$293
General Public Safety	7TAC76	774.25625	$F7E	804.25625	$293
General Public Safety	7TAC76D	774.25625	$F7E	774.25625	$293
Other Public Safety	7GTAC77	774.85625	$F7E	804.85625	$293
Other Public Safety	7GTAC77D	774.85625	$F7E	774.85625	$293
Mobile Repeater	7MOB79	774.50625	$F7E	804.50625	$293
Mobile Repeater	7MOB79D	774.50625	$F7E	774.50625	$293
Law Enforcement	7LAW81	774.00625	$F7E	804.00625	$293
Law Enforcement	7LAW81D	774.00625	$F7E	774.00625	$293
Law Enforcement	7LAW82	774.35625	$F7E	804.35625	$293
Law Enforcement	7LAW82D	774.35625	$F7E	774.35625	$293

- Authorized emission – 8K10F1E (Digital P25 Phase I Modulation) – 47 CFR §90.548(a)(1)
- Utilize normal squelch in programming which will use the default talkgroup - $0001 ($1_{10}$).
- AES Encryption permitted on all but the two nationwide interoperability calling channel. Must have accessible switch or other readily accessible control that permits the radio user to disable encryption. 47 CFR §90.553

700 MHz Nationwide Interoperability Channels

Assignment	Channel Name	Mobile RX Freq. (MHz)	Mobile RX CTCSS/NAC	Mobile TX Freq. (MHz)	Mobile TX CTCSS/NAC
Fire	7FIRE83	773.50625	$F7E	803.50625	$293
Fire	7FIRE83D	773.50625	$F7E	773.50625	$293
Fire	7FIRE84	773.85625	$F7E	803.85625	$293
Fire	7FIRE84D	773.85625	$F7E	773.85625	$293
EMS	7MED86	773.00625	$F7E	803.00625	$293
EMS	7MED86D	773.00625	$F7E	773.00625	$293
EMS	7MED87	773.35625	$F7E	803.35625	$293
EMS	7MED87D	773.35625	$F7E	773.35625	$293
Mobile Data *	7DATA89	774.75625	$F7E	804.75625	$293
Mobile Data *	7DATA89D	774.75625	$F7E	774.75625	$293

- Authorized emission – 8K10F1E (Digital P25 Phase I Modulation) – 47 CFR §90.548(a)(1)
- Utilize normal squelch in programming which will use the default talkgroup - $0001 ($1_{10}$).
- AES Encryption permitted on all but the two nationwide interoperability calling channel. Must have accessible switch or other readily accessible control that permits the radio user to disable encryption. 47 CFR §90.553
* Voice communications are permitted on 7DATA89 / 7DATA869D on a secondary basis – 90.531(b)(1)(i).

700 MHz Nationwide Air-Ground Channels

LICENSING REQUIRED: These frequencies are NOT covered by the "Blanket Authorization" for nationwide interoperability channels. Use of these channels must be licensed or authorized by STA.

Assignment	Channel Name	Mobile RX Freq. (MHz)	Mobile RX CTCSS/NAC	Mobile TX Freq. (MHz)	Mobile TX CTCSS/NAC
Air – Ground	7AG58	769.13125	$F7E	799.13125	$293
Air – Ground	7AG58D	769.13125	$F7E	769.13125	$293
Air – Ground	7AG60	769.63125	$F7E	799.63125	$293
Air – Ground	7AG60D	769.63125	$F7E	769.63125	$293
Air – Ground	7AG67	770.13125	$F7E	800.13125	$293
Air – Ground	7AG67D	770.13125	$F7E	770.13125	$293
Air – Ground	7AG68	770.63125	$F7E	800.63125	$293
Air – Ground	7AG68D	770.63125	$F7E	770.63125	$293

TX NAC: $293 ($659_{10}$), RX NAC $F7E ($3966_{10}$). These channels are reserved for air-ground communications to be used by low-altitude aircraft and ground-based stations: See FCC rule 90.531(7). (i) Airborne use of these channels is limited to aircraft flying at or below **457 meters (1500 feet) above ground level**. (ii) **Aircraft are limited to 2 watts effective radiated power (ERP)** when transmitting while airborne on these channels. (iii) Aircraft may transmit on either the mobile or base transmit side of the channel pair. (iv) States are responsible for the administration of these channels.
- Utilize normal squelch in programming which will use the default talkgroup - $0001 ($1_{10}$).

700 MHz Nationwide Air-Ground Channels

LICENSING REQUIRED: These frequencies are NOT covered by the "Blanket Authorization" for nationwide interoperability channels. Use of these channels must be licensed or authorized by STA.

Assignment	Channel Name	Mobile RX Freq. (MHz)	Mobile RX CTCSS/NAC	Mobile TX Freq. (MHz)	Mobile TX CTCSS/NAC
Air – Ground	7AG78	773.11875	$F7E	803.11875	$293
Air – Ground	7AG78D	773.11875	$F7E	773.11875	$293
Air – Ground	7AG80	773.61875	$F7E	803.61875	$293
Air – Ground	7AG80D	773.61875	$F7E	773.61875	$293
Air – Ground	7AG85	774.11875	$F7E	804.11875	$293
Air – Ground	7AG85D	774.11875	$F7E	774.11875	$293
Air – Ground	7AG88	774.61875	$F7E	804.61875	$293
Air – Ground (LZ)*	7AG88D	774.61875	$F7E	774.61875	$293

* 7AG88D is recommended for Landing Zone use.

TX NAC: $293 ($659_{10}$). RX NAC $F7E ($3966_{10}$). These channels are reserved for air-ground communications to be used by low-altitude aircraft and ground-based stations: See FCC rule 90.531(7). (i) Airborne use of these channels is limited to aircraft flying at or below **457 meters (1500 feet) above ground level.** (ii) **Aircraft are limited to 2 watts effective radiated power (ERP)** when transmitting while airborne on these channels. (iii) Aircraft may transmit on either the mobile or base transmit side of the channel pair. (iv) States are responsible for the administration of these channels.

- Utilize normal squelch in programming which will use the default talkgroup - $0001 ($1_{10}$).

700 MHz Low Power Itinerant Channels

LICENSING REQUIRED: These frequencies are NOT covered by the "Blanket Authorization" for nationwide interoperability channels. Use of these channels must be licensed or authorized by STA.

Assignment	Channel Name	Mobile RX Freq. (MHz)	Mobile RX CTCSS/NAC	Mobile TX Freq. (MHz)	Mobile TX CTCSS/NAC
Low Power - PS	7-US-01	769.05625	156.7 / $F7E	799.05625	156.7 / $293
Low Power - PS	7-US-01D	769.05625	156.7 / $F7E	769.05625	156.7 / $293
Low Power - PS	7-US-02	769.06875	156.7 / $F7E	799.06875	156.7 / $293
Low Power - PS	7-US-02D	769.06875	156.7 / $F7E	769.06875	156.7 / $293
Low Power - PS	7-US-03	774.99375	156.7 / $F7E	804.99375	156.7 / $293
Low Power - PS	7-US-03D	774.99375	156.7 / $F7E	774.99375	156.7 / $293

LICENSING NOTES: These channels may be licensed for national itinerant mobile use, use station class MOI. These channels may be used in either Analog or Digital mode and are limited to 2 watts (ERP).
- Licensees are responsible for the administration of these channels.
- Utilize normal squelch in programming which will use the default talkgroup - $0001 ($1_{10}$).

700 MHz Nationwide Deployable Trunked System Channels

LICENSING REQUIRED: These frequencies are NOT covered by the "Blanket Authorization" for nationwide interoperability channels. Use of these channels must be licensed or authorized by STA.

Common Nationwide System ID:
$101 ($257_{10}$)

Common Nationwide WACN:
$BF7CC

"$" Indicates hexadecimal value, "10" subscript indicates decimal value.

Assignment	Channel Name	Mobile RX Freq. (MHz)	Mobile RX CTCSS/NAC	Mobile TX Freq. (MHz)	Mobile TX CTCSS/NAC
	A	769.23125	——	799.23125	——
	B	769.38125	——	799.38125	——
	C*	769.73125	——	799.73125	——
	D*	769.88125	——	799.88125	——
Primary Control Channel	E	774.51875	——	804.51875	——
Secondary Control Channel	F	774.86875	——	804.86875	——

*Not available for use above the A-Line in Pennsylvania, New York, and Vermont.

- NRPC is the curator of the common nationwide system keys. To apply for system keys, contact the NRPC: nrpc.us
- Additional working channels separate from this list can be allocated locally to deployable systems subject to individual RPC approval.
- Each deployable trunk system should coordinate their unique NAC Code with the NRPC.

54

700 MHz Nationwide Deployable Trunked System Talkgroups

Recommended Talkgroups - Zone "YY DEPLOY" – System ID $101

	Channel Name	Eligible Users / Usage	TG Decimal ID	TG Hex ID
1	CALL YY	Calling / Initial Contact TG	201	$C9
2	CMD YY	Pre-designated Command TG	202	$CA
3	TAC YY3	General / Tactical Use TG	203	$CB
4	TAC YY4	General / Tactical Use TG	204	$CC
5	TAC YY5	General / Tactical Use TG	205	$CD
6	TAC YY6	General / Tactical Use TG	206	$CE
7	TAC YY7	General / Tactical Use TG	207	$CF
8	TAC YY8	General / Tactical Use TG	208	$D0

- Each deployable trunk system should coordinate their unique NAC Code with the NRPC.
- Duplicate unit ID's with deployable trunked radio systems are a possibility. Subscriber programming resources may be needed to mitigate duplicate ID's.

700 MHz Nationwide Deployable Trunked System Talkgroups

Recommended Talkgroups - Zone "YY DEPLOY" – System ID $101

	Channel Name	Eligible Users / Usage	TG Decimal ID	TG Hex ID
9	TAC YY9	General / Tactical Use TG	209	$D1
10	TAC YY10	General / Tactical Use TG	210	$D2
11	TAC YY11	General / Tactical Use TG	211	$D3
12	TAC YY12	General / Tactical Use TG	212	$D4
13	TAC YY13	General / Tactical Use TG	213	$D5
14	TAC YY14	General / Tactical Use TG	214	$D6
15	TAC YY15	General / Tactical Use TG	215	$D7
16	EMER YY	EMERGENCY USE TG	216	$D8

- Each deployable trunk system should coordinate their unique NAC Code with the NRPC.
- Duplicate unit ID's with deployable trunked radio systems are a possibility. Subscriber programming resources may be needed to mitigate duplicate ID's.

700 MHz Nationwide Deployable Trunked System Talkgroups

Recommended Talkgroups - Zone "ZZ DEPLOY" – System ID $101

	Channel Name	Eligible Users / Usage	TG Decimal ID	TG Hex ID
1	CALL ZZ	Calling / Initial Contact TG	101	$65
2	CMD ZZ	Pre-designated Command TG	102	$66
3	TAC ZZ3	General / Tactical Use TG	103	$67
4	TAC ZZ4	General / Tactical Use TG	104	$68
5	TAC ZZ5	General / Tactical Use TG	105	$69
6	TAC ZZ6	General / Tactical Use TG	106	$6A
7	TAC ZZ7	General / Tactical Use TG	107	$6B
8	TAC ZZ8	General / Tactical Use TG	108	$6C

- Each deployable trunk system should coordinate their unique NAC Code with the NRPC.
- Duplicate unit ID's with deployable trunked radio systems are a possibility. Subscriber programming resources may be needed to mitigate duplicate ID's.

700 MHz Nationwide Deployable Trunked System Talkgroups

Recommended Talkgroups - Zone "ZZ DEPLOY" – System ID $101

	Channel Name	Eligible Users / Usage	TG Decimal ID	TG Hex ID
9	TAC ZZ9	General / Tactical Use TG	109	$6D
10	TAC ZZ10	General / Tactical Use TG	110	$6E
11	TAC ZZ11	General / Tactical Use TG	111	$6F
12	TAC ZZ12	General / Tactical Use TG	112	$70
13	TAC ZZ13	General / Tactical Use TG	113	$71
14	TAC ZZ14	General / Tactical Use TG	114	$72
15	TAC ZZ15	General / Tactical Use TG	115	$73
16	EMER ZZ	EMERGENCY USE TG	116	$74

- Each deployable trunk system should coordinate their unique NAC Code with the NRPC.
- Duplicate unit ID's with deployable trunked radio systems are a possibility. Subscriber programming resources may be needed to mitigate duplicate ID's.

800 MHz Nationwide Interoperability Channels

Assignment	Channel Name	Mobile RX Freq. (MHz)	Mobile RX CTCSS/NAC	Mobile TX Freq. (MHz)	Mobile TX CTCSS/NAC
Calling	8CALL90	851.0125	156.7	806.0125	156.7
Calling - Direct	8CALL90D	851.0125	156.7	851.0125	156.7
Tactical	8TAC91	851.5125	156.7	806.5125	156.7
Tactical - Direct	8TAC91D	851.5125	156.7	851.5125	156.7
Tactical	8TAC92	852.0125	156.7	807.0125	156.7
Tactical - Direct	8TAC92D	852.0125	156.7	852.0125	156.7
Tactical	8TAC93	852.5125	156.7	807.5125	156.7
Tactical - Direct	8TAC93D	852.5125	156.7	852.5125	156.7
Tactical	8TAC94	853.0125	156.7	808.0125	156.7
Tactical - Direct	8TAC94D	853.0125	156.7	853.0125	156.7

- Recommended authorized emission – 14K0F3E (4.0 kHz deviation NPSPAC analog FM) – 47 CFR §90.617(a)(1) and 47 CFR §90.619(a)(5)(i). The FCC rules allow 5 KHz deviation for the 8CALL / 8TAC interoperability channels - 47 CFR §90.209(b)(5). Some Regional Planning Committees (RPCs) may limit their region to 4kHz.
- Encryption may not be used – 47 CFR §90.20(i)

P25 Digital Codes

NAC – Network Access Codes

293 (659_{10})	Default NAC
$F7E$ (3966_{10})	Receiver will un-squelch with any incoming NAC
$F7F$ (3967_{10})	A repeater with this NAC will allow incoming signals to be repeated with the NAC intact

TGID – Talkgroup ID

0001 (1_{10})	Default TGID, should be used in systems where no other talkgroups are defined
0000 (0_{10})	No-one or a talkgroup with no users – used for individual call
$FFFF$ (65535_{10})	Reserved as a talkgroup which includes everyone

UID – Unit ID

000000	No-one. This value is never assigned to a radio unit
000001-$98767F$	For general use.
989680-$FFFFFE$	For talk group use or other special purposes.
$FFFFFF$	Designates everyone – used when implementing a group call with a TGID

Note: Project 25 System Administrators should be aware of possible Unit ID conflicts when conducting operations with neighboring jurisdictions. System administrators should coordinate Unit IDs with agencies likely to operate on their system(s) to address any radio Unit ID conflicts.

"$" indicates hexadecimal values, "10" subscript indicates decimal value.

Continuous Tone-Coded Squelch System – CTCSS, Codes, & NAC Conversions

Freq. (Hz)	Motorola Code	NAC Conv	NIFC & CA Fire *	Freq. (Hz)	Motorola Code	NAC Conv	NIFC & CA Fire *	Freq. (Hz)	Motorola Code	NAC Conv	NIFC & CA Fire *
67.0	XZ	$29E	17	107.2	1B	$430	10	173.8	6A	$6CA	29
69.3**	WZ	$2B5	—	110.9	2Z	$455	1	179.9	6B	$707	30
71.9	XA	$2CF	18	114.8	2A	$47C	11	186.2	7Z	$746	31
74.4	WA	$2E8	19	118.8	2B	$4A4	28	192.8	7A	$788	16
77.0	XB	$302	20	123.0	3Z	$4CE	2	203.5	M1	$7F3	32
79.7	WB	$31D	21	127.3	3A	$4F9	12	206.5	8Z	$811	—
82.5	YZ	$339	22	131.8	3B	$526	3	210.7	M2	$83B	—
85.4	YA	$356	23	136.5	4Z	$555	4	218.1	M3	$885	—
88.5	YB	$375	24	141.3	4A	$585	13	225.7	M4	$8D1	—
91.5	ZZ	$393	25	146.2	4B	$5B6	5	229.1	9Z	$8F3	—
94.8	ZA	$3B4	26	151.4	5Z	$5EA	14	233.6	M5	$920	—
97.4	ZB	$3CE	27	156.7	5A	$61F	6	241.8	M6	$972	—
100.0	1Z	$3E8	9	162.2	5B	$656	15	250.3	M7	$9C7	—
103.5	1A	$40B	8	167.9	6Z	$68F	7	254.1	0Z	$9ED	—

- NAC Conversion – "$" indicates hexadecimal value.

*California FIRESCOPE tone list, used by NIFC and CA Fire Agencies.

Reference: firescope.caloes.ca.gov/ICS%20Documents/2020%20MACS-441-1.pdf

** 69.4 in some radios

Continuous Digital-Coded Squelch System - CDCSS Codes

Normal	Inverted	Nor.	Inv.	Nor.	Inv.	Nor.	Inv.	Nor.	Inv.	Nor.	Inv.
023	047	116	754	212*	356	306	071	432	516	565	703
025	244	122*	225	223	134	311	664	445	043	606	631
026	464	125	365	225*	122	315	423	446*	255	612	346
031	627	131	364	226	411	325*	526	452*	053	624	632
036*	172	132	546	243	251	331	465	454*	266	627	031
043	445	134	223	244	025	332*	455	455*	332	631	606
047	023	143	412	245	072	343	532	462*	252	632	324
051	032	145*	274	246*	523	346	612	464	026	654	743
053*	452	152	115	251	165	351	243	465	331	662	466
054	413	032	051	252*	462	364	131	466	662	664	311
065	271	155	731	255*	446	365	125	503	162	703	565
071	306	156	265	261	732	371	734	506	073	712	114
072	245	162	503	263	205	411	226	516	432	723	431
073	506	165	251	265	156	412	143	523*	246	731	155
074	174	172	036	266*	454	413	054	526*	325	732	261
114	712	174	074	271	065	423	315	532	343	734	271
115	152	205	263	274*	145	431	723	546	132	743	654
										754	116

* This Code is not standard amongst sampling of 12 different radios checked.

Federal / Non-Federal SAR Command Interoperability Plan

	Channel Name	Mobile RX Freq. (MHz)	Mobile RX CTCSS/NAC	Mobile TX Freq. (MHz)	Mobile TX CTCSS/NAC
Connect with Gateway	IR 12*	410.8375	CSQ	419.8375	167.9
	VTAC14	159.4725	156.7	159.4725	156.7
	UTAC43	453.8625	156.7	458.8625	156.7
	8TAC94	853.0125	156.7	808.0125	156.7
	VHF Marine Ch. 17**	156.8500	CSQ	156.8500	—

- This table does not convey authority to operate.
- Always monitor and verify the channels are not in use prior to operating.
- If a repeater is not available, substitute the corresponding talk-around channel: IR 18 for IR 12, UTAC43D for UTAC43, 8TAC94D for 8TAC94.

*See Conditions for Use of Federal Interoperability Channels on pages 19-22.

**Use of VHF Marine Ch. 17 requires an FCC STA and use emission – 16K0F3E (5 kHz deviation wideband analog FM).

Federal / Non-Federal VHF SAR Operations Interoperability Plan

Direction from USCG, FCC, or FAA overrides information in this table. This table does not convey authority to operate.

Suggested SAR Function	Frequency (MHz)
Ground Operations	155.1600 MHz (VSAR16 – License Required) 2.5 kHz deviation narrowband analog FM
Maritime Operations *	157.0500 MHz or 157.1500 MHz (VHF Marine 21A or 23A) as specified by USCG Sector Commander
Air Operations - civilian	123.100 MHz AM (may not be used for tests or exercises)
Air Operations – USCG/Military	345.0 MHz AM for initial contact only, then move to 282.8 MHz AM or other working channel
Air rescue assets to air rescue assets (deconfliction)	As charted on standard air chart or MULTICOM 122.850 MHz (south or west sector) & 122.900 MHz (north or east sector), or as specified by FAA. 122.850 MHz may not be used for tests or exercises.
Ground to Air SAR Working Channel	157.1750 MHz VHF Marine 83A (21A, 23A, or 81A alternates as specified by local USCG Sector Commander **)
Ground to Maritime SAR working channel	157.0500 MHz VHF Marine 21A (23A, 81A, or 83A alternates as specified by local USCG Sector Commander **)
Maritime/Air/Ground SAR working channel *	157.1750 MHz VHF Marine 83A (21A, 23A, or 81A are alternates as specified by local USCG Sector Commander **)
EMS/Medical Support	155.3400 MHz (VMED28 – License Required) 2.5 kHz deviation narrowband analog FM
Hailing* & DISTRESS only – Maritime/Air/Ground	156.8000 MHz VHF Marine 16 *

- VHF marine channels use emission 16KOF3E (5 kHz deviation analog FM).
* Use VHF Marine Ch.16 to make contact (30 seconds max.), then move to appropriate working channel as directed by local USCG Sector Commander. Non-maritime use of any VHF Marine channel requires FCC Special Temporary Authority or appropriate license.
** VHF Marine channels: 16=156.8000 21A=157.0500 22A=157.1000 23A=157.1500 81A=157.0750 82A=157.1250 83A=157.1750

Common Emission Designators in Public Safety Licensing

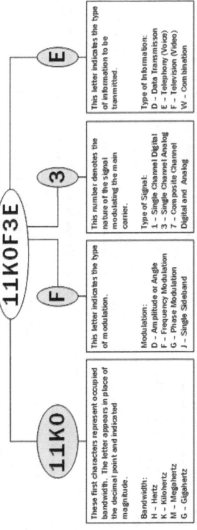

11K0F3E

11K0 — These first characters represent occupied bandwidth. The letter appears in place of the decimal point and indicated magnitude.

Bandwidth:
H – Hertz
K – Kilohertz
M – Megahertz
G – Gigahertz

F — This letter indicates the type of modulation.

Modulation:
D – Amplitude or Angle
F – Frequency Modulation
G – Phase Modulation
J – Single Sideband

3 — This number denotes the nature of the signal modulating the main carrier.

Type of Signal:
1 – Single Channel Digital
3 – Single Channel Analog
7 – Composite Channel
Digital and Analog

E — This letter indicates the type of information to be tranmitted.

Type of Information:
D – Data Transmission
E – Telephony (Voice)
F – Television (Video)
W – Combination

Emission	Description
150HA1A	Continuous Wave Telegraphy
2K8OJ3E	SSB, Suppressed Carrier, Voice
8K10F1D	P25 Phase 1 Digital, Data
8K10F1E	P25 Phase 1 Digital, Voice
8K30F1W	P25 Phase 1 Digital, Voice & Data

Emission	Description
11K0F3D	2.5 kHz Analog FM, Data (DTMF)
11K0F3E	2.5 kHz Analog FM, Voice (Narrow)
14K0F3E	4.0 kHz Analog FM, Voice (NPSPAC)
16K0F3E	5.0 kHz Analog FM, Voice (Wide)
30M0D7W	Microwave Link, 2048 QAM

FCC Part 90 Common Station Class Codes

Station Class	Station Class Description	Examples
FB	Base	Fixed Location Base Radio at a specific location authorized to communicate with mobile stations
FB2	Mobile Relay	Fixed Location Repeater – Conventional, decentralized trunking, or centralized trunking (frequency band specific)
FB4	Community Repeater	Fixed Location Repeater – Conventional operating with multiple CTCSS or CDCSS
FB8	Centralized Trunked Relay	Trunked Radio Systems below 512 MHz
FB2T	Mobile Relay – Temporary	Mobile, Temporary or Tactical Repeaters
FX1	Control (Control Station)	Fixed location base radio that operates through a mobile relay (repeater) in the same way a mobile station operates
6.1	Control (Control Station)	Control Station – Antenna height below 20 ft to tip (6.1 Meters)
MO	Mobile	Handheld and vehicular mounted radios intended to be used while in motion or during halts at unspecified points
MOI	Mobile - Itinerant	A similar station class to mobile (MO), but no interference protection is provided from other itinerant operations.
MO3	Mobile/Vehicular Repeater	Simplex radio attached to a vehicular mounted radio to extend range
MO8	Centralized Trunk Mobile	Handheld and Vehicular Mounted Radios operating on trunked radio systems below 512 MHz

Line-of-Sight Formulas

Earth's Curvature
Approximately 8 inches (7.98) per Mile

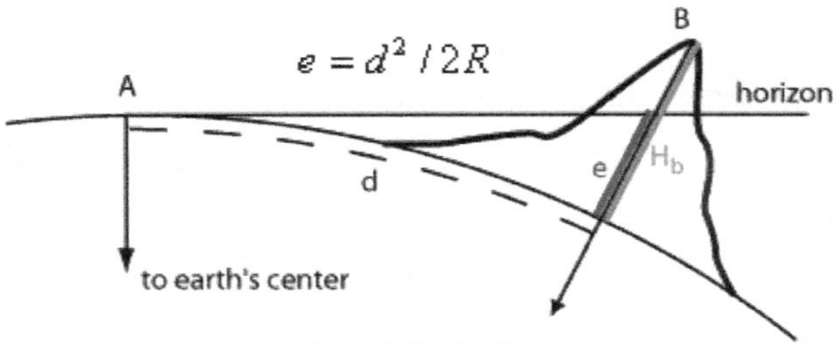

$$e = d^2 / 2R$$

Visual Line-of-Sight
Approximate distance in miles = 1.33 × √ (height in feet)

Radio Line-of-Sight
$D = √(2Hr) + √(2Ht)$

Where:

D = approximate distance (range) to radio horizon in miles
Hr = height of receive antenna in feet
Ht = height of transmit antenna in feet

Figure 2: Earth's Curvature

These are rough estimates that only consider the curvature of the earth, which does not take into account power, antenna type, antenna gain, frequency, clutter, terrain or other obstructions.

Range (miles)	8	10	11	12	13	16	17	21	23	28	32	35	42	48
Tx Ant. Height (ft)	10	20	30	40	50	75	100	150	200	300	400	500	750	1000
Rx Ant. Height (ft)	5.5	5.5	5.5	5.5	5.5	5.5	5.5	5.5	5.5	5.5	5.5	5.5	5.5	5.5

25 Cities Project Federal Interoperability Channels

The 25 Cities Federal Interoperability Channels are VHF channels that use FBI fixed infrastructure to provide wide area coverage for federal, state, and local public safety users. There are currently 56 channels, overseen by 31 FBI Field Offices. The primary use of the channels is for interoperable communications during both pre-planned and emergency events. The channels may also be available for internal agency communications. All pre-planned use must be coordinated with the local FBI Telecommunications Manager. All federal, state, and local public safety agencies are encouraged to program the 25 Cities frequencies into their land mobile radio subscriber devices.

Most 25 Cities VHF channels are accessible by non-VHF users via permanent or ad hoc patching capabilities provided to many agencies as part of the 25 Cities Project. Please note that in certain cities, the channels use the VHF Law Enforcement (LE) Federal Interoperability frequencies: Baltimore (BA LE 3); Boston (BS LE 4); Charlotte (CE LE 4); Honolulu (HNL LE 2, HNL LE 3, HNL LE 4, HNL LE 5); Kansas City (KC FIOLE2); Milwaukee (MW LE 4, MW LE3 GB, MW LE2 MA); Newark (NK FIO LE 2); Richmond (RH LE4); San Juan/Puerto Rico (SJ LE 2 ME, SJ LE 3 YQ, SJ LE 4 CS, SJ LE 5 CP, and SJ LE 2 STT), and Washington, D.C. (DC LE 2).

To program the channels, please request the complete list of 25 Cities frequencies from the 25 Cities Program Manager:

Brian Zuniga, DOJ / FBI
703-985-1165
BOZUNIGA@FBI.GOV

For specific information about a particular channel, please contact the FBI Telecommunications Manager, at the provided FBI Field Office telephone number.

25 Cities Project Federal Interoperability Channels

Field Office	CHANNEL(S) DESCRIPTION	MAIN FBI OFFICE NUMBER / REQUEST FBI TELECOMMUNI-CATIONS MANAGER
ATLANTA	**ATL FIO** VHF P25 350 watt voted repeater system - 4 receive sites	770-216-3000
BALTIMORE	**BA LE 3** VHF P25 350 watt voted repeater system - 5 receive sites	410-265-8080
BOSTON	**BPD FIO** VHF narrowband analog 125 watt voted repeater system - 15 receive sites	857-386-2000
BOSTON	**BS LE 4 / BK FIO** VHF P25 multicast 1 x 350 watt (BS LE 4) and 1 x 125 watt (BK FIO) [Brockton, MA] voted repeater system - 7 receive sites	
CHARLOTTE	**CE LE 4** VHF P25 125 watt standalone repeater	704-672-6100
CHICAGO	**CGCOM-N / CGCOM-C / CGCOM-S** (Lake Zurich / Chicago / Joliet) VHF P25 multicast 3 x 125 watt voted repeater systems - 20 receive sites	312-421-6700

City	Channels / Description	Phone
CHICAGO	**CGTAC-N / CGTAC-C / CGTAC-S** (Lake Zurich / Chicago / Joliet) VHF P25 multicast 3 x 125 watt voted repeater systems -20 receive sites	312-421-6700
DALLAS	**DFW-E** (Dallas) VHF P25 350 watt voted repeater system - 9 receive sites	972-559-5000
DALLAS	**DFW-W** (Ft. Worth) VHF P25 350 watt voted repeater system - 7 receive sites	
DENVER	**DEN IO-N / DEN IO-E / DEN IO-C / DEN IO-S / DEN IO-W** (Thorton/ Smoky Hill / Central Denver / RCFL / Fed Center) VHF P25 multicast 5 x 125 watt voted repeater system	303-629-7171
DETROIT	**8TAC 92** *800 MHz wideband analog standalone repeater*	313-965-2323
DETROIT	**8TAC 94** *800 MHz wideband analog standalone repeater*	
EL PASO	**ELP FIO-W / ELP FIO-E** (El Paso / Sierra Blanca) VHF P25 multicast 2 x 300 watt voted repeater system - no additional receive sites	915-832-5000

HONOLULU	**HNL FIO** VHF P25 125 watt standalone repeater	808-566-4300
HONOLULU	**HNL-PJKK-Federal Building-Downtown Honolulu** VHF P25 125 watt standalone repeater	
HONOLULU	**HNL FIO2-Western Oahu** VHF P25 125 watt standalone repeater	
HONOLULU	**HNL LE 2-Waikiki** VHF P25 125 watt standalone repeater	
HONOLULU	**HNL LE 3-Diamond Head** VHF P25 125 watt standalone repeater	
HONOLULU	**HNL LE 4-Deployable** VHF P25 125 watt transportable repeater	
HONOLULU	**HNL LE 5-HNL Airport** VHF P25 125 watt transportable repeater	
HOUSTON	**HOU CMD** VHF P25 350 watt voted repeater systems--14 receive sites	713-693-5000
HOUSTON	**HOU PAT** VHF P25 350 watt voted repeater systems--14 receive sites	
JACKSONVILLE	**JAX FIO** VHF P25 350 watt voted repeater system - 8 receive sites	904-248-7000

KANSAS CITY	**KC LE 2** VHF P25 125 watt voted repeater system - 4 receive sites	816-512-8200
LOS ANGELES	**LA FIO1** VHF P25 350 watt voted repeater systems - 8 receive sites	
LOS ANGELES	**LA FIO2** VHF P25 350 watt voted repeater systems - 8 receive sites	310-477-6565
LOS ANGELES	**LA FIO3** VHF P25 350 watt voted repeater systems - 8 receive sites	
MIAMI	**MIA FIO** VHF P25 350 watt voted repeater system - 14 receive sites	754-703-2000
MILWAUKEE	**MW LE 4** VHF P25 350 watt voted repeater system - 3 receive sites	
MILWAUKEE	**BELOIT - MW LE3 BE** VHF P25 125 watt standalone repeater	
MILWAUKEE	**GREEN BAY - MW LE3 GB** VHF P25 125 watt standalone repeater	414-276-4684
MILWAUKEE	**MADISON - MW LE2 MA** VHF P25 125-watt standalone repeater	
MINNEAPOLIS	**FED-MP / FED-SP** (Minneapolis / St. Paul) VHF P25 multicast 1 x 350 watt (FED-MP) and 1 x 125 watt (FED-SP) voted repeater system - 9 receive sites	763-569-8000

Location	Description	Phone
NEW HAVEN	**CFedcom-N / CFedcom-S / CFedcom-E / CFedcom-W** (Avon / Hamden / Bozrah / Redding) VHF P25 multicast 4 x 125 watt voted repeater system - 12 receive sites	203-777-6311
NEW ORLEANS	**NOLA FIO** VHF P25 350 watt voted repeater system - 13 receive sites	504-816-3000
NEW YORK	**NYC FIO / NYC FIO-N / NYC FIO-E / NYC FIO-S** (NYC / Orange-Putnam / Suffolk County / Central NJ) VHF P25 multicast 3 x 350 watt voted repeater system 1 x 125 watt (NYC FIO-E / Suffolk) - 32 receive sites	212-384-1000
NEW YORK	**NYC FED IO 2** VHF P25 350 watt voted repeater system - 14 receive sites	
NEWARK NJ	**NK FIO LE 2** VHF P25 350 watt voted repeater system - 12 receive sites	973-792-3000
NORFOLK	**HRN FIOP DRI / HRN FIOP TOA** (Suffolk-Driver / Toano) VHF P25 multicast 1 x 350 watt [Suffolk-Driver], 1 x 125 watt [Toano] voted repeater system - 10 receive sites	757-455-0100
ORLANDO (RA-Tampa FO)	**ORL FIO** VHF P25 350 watt voted repeater system - 9 receive sites	813-253-1000
PHILADELPHIA	**PH FIO** VHF P25 350 watt voted repeater system - 12 receive sites	215-418-4000

RICHMOND VA	RH LE4 / RH FIO (Midlothian / Petersburg) VHF P25 multicast 1 x 350 watt (RH LE 4) [Midlothian] and 1 x 100 watt (RH FIO) [Petersburg] voted repeater system - 8 receive sites	804-261-1044
SAN DIEGO	**CALAW1** VHF narrowband analog simplex voted receive systems with transmitters controlled by RCS dispatcher. 9 receive sites	858-320-5380
SAN DIEGO	**VLAW31** VHF narrowband analog simplex voted receive systems with transmitters controlled by RCS dispatcher. 9 receive sites	
SAN DIEGO	**CALAW8** 800 MHz analog NPSPAC standard (16K0F3E) simplex voted receive systems with transmitters controlled by RCS dispatcher. 10 receive sites	
SAN DIEGO	**CAFIRE1** 800 MHz analog NPSPAC standard (16K0F3E) simplex voted receive systems with transmitters controlled by RCS dispatcher- 10 receive sites	

SAN FRANCISCO	**SF FED-ED / SF FED-ES / SF FED-ET / SF FED-EW** (Diablo / San Bruno / Tam / Weideman) VHF P25 multicast 4 x 125 watt voted repeater system - 10 receive sites	415-553-7400
SAN FRANCISCO	**SF MA-V / SF MA-U** (Twin Peaks) 1X VHF P25, 1X UHF P25 125 watt standalone repeaters. These two repeaters are cross-banded together	
SAN FRANCISCO	**SF FED-V / SF FED-U** (Twin Peaks) 1X VHF P25, 1X UHF P25 125 watt standalone repeaters. These two repeaters are cross-banded together	
SAN JUAN	**SJ LE 2 ME / SJ LE 3 YQ / SJ LE 4 CS / SJ LE 5 CP / SJ LE 2 STT** (Monte del Estado Maricao / El Yunque Peak / Cerro La Santa Telemundo Tower / Cerro Punta Claro Building / St Thomas-Crown Mountain) VHF P25 multicast 3 x 350 watt (SJ LE 2 ME / SJ LE 3 YQ / SJ LE 5 CP) and 2 x 110 watt (SJ LE 4 CS / SJ LE 2 STT[St. Thomas]) repeater system. Multicast-- Inputs at every site are rebroadcast at every other site. SJ LE 3 YQ - 1 receive site, SJ LE 5 CP - 1 receive site, SJ LE 2 ME - 3 receive sites [planned]	787-754-6000

Location	System	Description	Phone
ST LOUIS *	**STL CALL**	VHF P25 350 watt voted repeater systems, 9 receive sites	314-589-2500
ST LOUIS *	**STL TAC**	VHF P25 350 watt voted repeater systems, 9 receive sites	
TAMPA	**TAM FIO**	VHF P25 350 watt voted repeater system - 7 receive sites	813-253-1000
WASHINGTON DC	**DC IO-1**	VHF P25 350 watt voted repeater system - 9 receive sites	202-278-2000
WASHINGTON DC	**DC LE 2**	VHF P25 350 watt voted repeater system - 9 receive sites	
NORTH AMERICAN SATELLITE	**J-SMART - Talkgroup #15** Ligado Satellite Interoperability Talkgroup MSAT Satellite Radio PTT/one-to-many		1-888-664-6727 Network Innovations

Encryption – National Reserved SLN Table

The National Law Enforcement Communications Center (NLECC), a subdivision of Customs and Border Protection, generates and distributes national interoperability keys for Slot Location Numbers (SLNs) 1-20.

Any agencies that plan on utilizing encryption as part of their interoperability plans should contact their SWIC for guidance (cisa.gov/safecom/ncswic-membership). Encryption key management is the administration of policies and procedures for protecting, storing, organizing, and distributing encryption keys. Effective encryption key management is crucial as it ensures that encryption does not impede the operability or interoperability of radio system users.

Documents outlining best practices can be found at: cisa.gov/safecom/blog/2016/10/12/fpic-releases-encryption-documents or by contacting CISA through your SWIC.

National Reserved Slot Location Numbers (SLN)					
SLN	ALG	Use	SLN Name	Crypto Period	Authorized Users
1	DES	Public Safety Interoperable	ALL IO D	Annual	All Network Users
2	DES	Federal Interoperable	FED IO D	Annual	All Federal Network Users
3	AES	Public Safety Interoperable	ALL IO A	Annual	All Network Users
4	AES	Federal Interoperable	FED IO A	Annual	All Federal Network Users
5	DES	National Law Enforcement State & Local	NLE IO D	Static	All Federal, State, and Local Law Enforcement
6	AES	National Law Enforcement State & Local	NLE IO A	Static	All Federal, State, and Local Law Enforcement
7	AES	US–Canadian Federal LE Interoperability	FED CAN	Static	All US & Canadian Federal LE
8	AES	US-Canadian Public Safety Interoperability	USCAN PS	Static	All US & Canadian PS Users

Encryption – National Reserved SLN Table - continued

9	DES	National Tactical Event	NTAC D	Single Event Use	All Federal, State, & Local Public Safety
10	AES	National Tactical Event	NTAC A	Single Event Use	All Federal, State, & Local Public Safety
11	DES	Multiple Public Safety Disciplines	PS IO D	Static	All Federal, State, & Local Public Safety
12	AES	Multiple Public Safety Disciplines	PS IO A	Static	All Federal, State, & Local Public Safety
13	DES	National Fire, EMS, & Rescue	NFER D	Static	All Fire, EMS, & Rescue Users
14	AES	National Fire, EMS, & Rescue	NFER A	Static	All Fire, EMS, & Rescue Users
15	DES	National Task Force Operations	FED TF D	One Time Usage	Federal Task Force
16	AES	National Task Force Operations	FED TF A	One Time Usage	Federal Task Force
17	DES	National Law Enforcement Task Force	NLE TF D	One Time Usage	All Federal, State and Local Law Enforcement
18	AES	National Law Enforcement Task Force	NLE TF A	One Time Usage	All Federal, State and Local Law Enforcement
19	AES	Fed–INTL LE Interoperability	FED INTL	When Needed	Federal and Visiting International LE
20	AES	Public Safety – INTL LE Interoperability	PS INTL	When Needed	All US and Visiting International Public Safety

Commonly Used Frequencies

Aviation Frequencies

AM Aviation Frequencies:

121.5	Emergency & Distress
123.1	Search and Rescue (SAR)
122.9	Search and Rescue (SAR) Secondary and Training

All frequencies on this page use AM (emission designator 6K00A3E). Emergency Position-Indicating Radio Beacons (EPIRB), Emergency Locator Transmitters (ELTs), and Personal Locator Beacons (PLBs) transmitters operate on 406.0 to 406.10 MHz, and some have low power 121.5 MHz homing beacons. Older ELTs use 121.5 MHz, which is also the civil aviation voice emergency frequency, and are still in widespread use.

Aviation Notes:

Communications with aircraft in the public safety environment is complex and carries additional risks over traditional land mobile radio. Communications occur in both AM and FM modes. AM communications are typically for pilot to pilot, pilot to tower, pilot to ARTCC, etc. It is less frequently used for tactical Air-to-Ground communications.

Extreme caution must be taken with AM Airband frequencies, these are the least desirable choice for Air-to-Ground communication. While not necessarily prohibited, it presents much greater risks to aviation assets than using a discrete Public Safety FM channel.

Most Air-to-Ground (A/G) communications occur on FM in the traditional FM VHF, UHF, 700 and 800 MHz bands. Careful coordination of these channels is critical. Frequencies coordinated specifically for that use should be employed.

Many jurisdictions have set aside or in some cases licensed specific Air to Ground FM channels in most of the bands. These allow the users to communicate with air assets in a safer environment.

A concern with any airborne transmitter is the extended range of the transmission when airborne. It is often the case that an aircraft can broadcast substantially further than the license limitations of the local licensee or user, possibly resulting in unintended interference to other agencies and to the aircraft itself.

When multiple aircraft operate in the same theatre of operations, frequency deconfliction and tasking coordination will prevent confusion.

Do not patch AM aviation frequencies without specific approval of each incident's Aviation Branch, or aviation knowledgeable personnel.

Notice to Airmen (NOTAM) Filing Instructions

File a Notice to Airmen (NOTAM) with the FAA to alert aircraft pilots of any hazards (such as a temporary tower or tethered antenna platform).

Filing Instructions:

1. Before calling FAA have Tower Registration number or ASR number, which is the 7-digit number assigned to the tower by the FCC (if available); and the nearest airport to tower.
2. Call **1-877-4-US-NTMS (1-877-487-6867)** - you will be prompted to enter state abbreviation (use letters on telephone keypad - page 137) or to verbally indicate a state.
3. Log the file number you will be given by the Flight Service Station (FSS) specialist.
4. NOTAMs are valid for 15 days and will expire unless a new NOTAM is filed. When filing a NOTAM for the erection of obstacles near airfields **including temporary heliports** it may be helpful to have the latitude, longitude, height above ground level, and type of obstruction lighting used (steady red, flashing etc.)

NOTAMs are issued (and reported) for a number of reasons, such as:

- hazards such as air-shows, parachute jumps, kite flying, lasers, rocket launches etc.
- inoperable radio navigational aids
- inoperable lights on tall obstructions
- temporary erection of obstacles near airfields (e.g., cranes, portable towers)

FAA NOTAMs, ARTCC Notices, TFRs and Special Notices

pilotweb.nas.faa.gov/PilotWeb/

Defense Internet NOTAM Service

notams.faa.gov/dinsQueryWeb/

Other FAA telephone numbers:
Flight Service Stations: 1-800-WX-BRIEF (1-800-992-7433)
FAA Main Number: 1-866-TELL-FAA (1-866-835-5322)

Unmanned Aircraft (UAS) Incident Reporting – Tips in Responding to a UAS Incident

D **Detect** all available elements of the situation. Look outward and upward to attempt to locate individuals who are holding a controller or device (laptop, notebook, cell phone) and appears to be operating a UAS. Look at windows, balconies, rooftops, and open spaces. For special events, predetermine likely locations that would enable a person to control at UAS.

R **Report Incident** to state or local law enforcement immediately and request a response if necessary. Execute organization's emergency response action plan if appropriate

O **Observe** the UAS and maintain visibility of the device. Look for the direction of travel, damage to facilities, and individuals. NOTE: Battery life is typically 20-30 minutes.

N **Notice features** and identify the type of device (i.e., Fixed-wing/Multi-rotor/Retail or Custom), size, shape, color, payload, video camera equipment, and activity.

E **Execute appropriate security/emergency response action** by maintaining a safe environment for the public and first responders in accordance with Federal, State, and local laws and regulations. Document event details including photo, if possible.

UAS Class and Category

Class	Visual	Category	Weight
Multi-Rotor		Micro/FPV	< .55 lbs
		Light	.55 – 3 lbs
		Medium	> 3 lbs to 10 lbs
		Heavy	> 10 lbs
Fixed-Wing		Light	< 4 lbs
		Heavy	> 4 lbs
Rotary-Wing		Light	< 10 lbs
		Heavy	> 10 lbs
Hybrid		Light	< 10 lbs
		Heavy	> 10 lbs

INCIDENT REPORTING
QUICK TIPS*

- Identify Operator and Witnesses
  (Name & Contact Info)
- Type of Incident/Operation
  (Commercial, Hobby, Public/Governmental)
- Type of Device(s) and UAS Registration Number
- Event Location and Incident Details
  (Date, Time, and Place)
- Evidence Collection
  (Photos, Videos, Device(s)

* Always follow state and local laws and regulations

faa.gov/uas/public_safety_gov/contacts/

82

UAS Frequency Reference

	UAS Frequency Reference		
Frequency Range	Frequency Type	Typical Power	Notes
27 MHz	Radio Controlled Vehicle		47 CFR Part 95, Subpart C 6 Discreet Frequencies
49 MHz	Radio Controlled Devices	< 100mW	47 CFR Part 15, Subpart C §15.235 5 Discreet Frequencies
50 MHz	Amateur (License Required)		47 CFR Part 97 10 Discreet Frequencies
53 MHz	Amateur (License Required)		47 CFR Part 97 8 Discreet Frequencies
72 MHz	Radio Controlled Aircraft	<750mW	47 CFR Part 95, Subpart C Reserved for "Aircraft" 50 Discreet Frequencies
75 MHz	Radio Controlled Vehicle	<750mW	47 CFR Part 95, Subpart C Reserved for "Surface" 30 Discreet Frequencies
431 MHz – 450 MHz	Amateur (License Required)	< 1000mW	47 CFR Part 97 Command & Control

UAS Frequency Reference

Frequency Range	Frequency Type	Typical Power	Notes
433 MHz	Industrial, Scientific, and Medical (ISM)	< 250mW	47 CFR Part 18 ISM is a secondary use of band
863 MHz – 870 MHz	European Short-Range Device	< 500mW	European allocations, some equipment may be being used illegally in the United States
902 MHz – 928 MHz	ISM	250 – 2,000mW	47 CFR Part 18 Video and Command & Control
1,240 MHz – 1,300 MHz	Amateur (License Required)	< 1,000mW	47 CFR Part 97 Video
2,300 MHz	Licensed	< 1,000mW	License Required
2,400 MHz – 2.4835 MHz	Wi-Fi	< 500mW	47 CFR, Part 15 Wi-Fi (2.4 GHz Band)
5,725 MHz – 5,825 MHz	Wi-Fi	< 500mW	47 CFR Part 15 Wi-Fi (5.8 GHz Band)

VHF Marine Channel Listing

This chart summarizes a portion of the FCC rules – 47 CFR §80.371(c) and §80.373(f)

Type of Message	Appropriate Channels *
DISTRESS SAFETY AND CALLING - Use this channel to get the attention of another station (calling) or in emergencies (distress and safety).	16
INTERSHIP SAFETY - Use this channel for ship-to-ship safety messages and for search and rescue messages to ships and aircraft of the Coast Guard.	6
COAST GUARD LIAISON - Use this channel to talk to the Coast Guard (but first make contact on Channel 16).	22A
COAST GUARD - These channels are Coast Guard working channels, not available to commercial or non-commercial vessels for normal use.	21A, 23A, 81A, 83A
U.S. Government - Environmental protection operations.	81A
U.S. Government - This channel is a working channel for U.S. Government vessels and U.S. Government coast stations only.	82A
NON-COMMERCIAL - Working channels for voluntary boats. Messages must be about the needs of the ship. Typical uses include fishing reports, rendezvous, scheduling repairs and berthing information. Use Channels 67 and 72 only for ship-to- ship messages.	9^6, 67^9, 68, 69, 71^8, 72, 78A, $79A^4$, $80A^4$

Type of Message	Appropriate Channels *
COMMERCIAL - Working channels for working ships only. Messages must be about business or the needs of the ship. Use channels 8, 67, 72 and 88 only for ship-to-ship messages.	01A^5, 07A, 8, 9, 10, 11, 18A, 19A, 63A^5, 67^7, 79A, 80A, 88^1
PUBLIC CORRESPONDENCE (MARINE OPERATOR) - Use these channels to call the marine operator at a public coast station. By contacting a public coast station, you can make and receive calls from telephones on shore. Except for distress calls, public coast stations usually charge for this service.	24, 25, 26, 27, 28, 84, 85, 86
PORT OPERATIONS - These channels are used in directing the movement of ships in or near ports, locks or waterways. Messages must be about the operational handling movement and safety of ships. In certain major ports, Channels 11, 12 and 14 are not available for general port operations messages. Use channel 20 only for ship-to-coast messages. Channel 77 is limited to intership communications to and from pilots.	01A^5, 05A^3, 12, 14, 20, 63A^5, 65A, 66A, 73, 74, 75^{10},76^{10}, 77
NAVIGATIONAL - (Also known as the bridge-to-bridge channel.) This channel is available to all ships. Messages must be about ship navigation, for example, passing or meeting other ships. You must keep your messages short. Your power output must not be more than one watt. This is also the main working channel at most locks and drawbridges.	13, 67

Type of Message	Appropriate Channels *
MARITIME CONTROL - This channel may be used to talk to ships and coast stations operated by state or local governments. Messages must pertain to regulation and control, boating activities, or assistance to ships.	17
DIGITAL SELECTIVE CALLING - Use this channel for distress and safety calling and for general purpose calling using only digital selective calling techniques.	70
WEATHER - On these channels you may receive weather broadcasts of the National Oceanic and Atmospheric Administration. These channels are only for receiving. You cannot transmit on them.	162.4000 Through 162.5500
Footnotes	
1. Not available in the Great Lakes, St. Lawrence Seaway, or the Puget Sound and the Strait of Juan de Fuca and its approaches.	
2. Only for use In the Great Lakes, St Lawrence Seaway, and Puget Sound and the Strait of Juan de Fuca and its approaches.	
3. Available only in the Houston and New Orleans areas.	
4. Available only in the Great Lakes.	
5. Available only in the New Orleans area.	
6. Available for Intership, ship, and coast general purpose calling by noncommercial ships.	
7. Available only In the Puget Sound and the Strait of Juan de Fuca.	

Type of Message	Appropriate Channels *
8. Available for port operations communications only within the U.S. Coast Guard designated VTS radio protection area of Seattle (Puget Sound). Normal output must not exceed 1 watt.	
9. Available for navigational communications only in the Mississippi River/Southwest Pass/Gulf outlet area.	
10. Available for navigation-related port operations or ship movement only. Output power limited to 1 watt.	
* NOTE - In older VHF marine radios, simplex channels with a "A" suffix are the same channels in newer VHF marine radios with "10" channel prefix which to indicate simplex use of the ship station transmit frequency of an international duplex channel. Example "01A" is the same as "1001". Used in U.S. waters only.	
October 9, 2019 Adapted from wireless.fcc.gov/bureau-divisions/mobility-division/ship-radio-stations	

Shipboard repeaters: 457.525 457.550 457.575 457.600 MHz

Inputs are +10.225 MHz (foreign vessels may use +10.0 MHz offset – not permitted in U.S. waters).

Maritime freqs. assignable to aircraft:

(HF) 2.738 2.830 3.023 4.125 5.680 MHz
(VHF) channels 6 8 9 16 18A 22A 67 68 72 & 88
See 47CFR §80.379 for restrictions.

Maritime Distress Frequencies - Radiotelephone

(HF, USB - 2K80J3E) 2182, 4125*, 6215*, 8291*, 12290*, 16420 kHz

* Note – The USCG has proposed the termination of monitoring these voice frequencies in favor of Digital Selective Calling (DSC) distress messages; except for Kodiak, AK and Guam.
(VHF, FM wideband 5 kHz deviation - 16K0F3E) 156.800 MHz (Channel 16)

VHF Marine Channels & Frequencies

Source: navcen.uscg.gov/?pageName=mtVhf

Channel Number *	Ship Transmit MHz	Ship Receive MHz	Use
01A	156.050	156.050	Port Operations and Commercial, VTS. Available only in New Orleans/Lower Mississippi area
05A	156.250	156.250	Port Operations or VTS in the Houston, New Orleans and Seattle areas
6	156.300	156.300	Intership Safety
07A	156.350	156.350	Commercial
8	156.400	156.400	Commercial (Intership only)
9	156.450	156.450	Boater Calling. Commercial and Non- Commercial
10	156.500	156.500	Commercial
11	156.550	156.550	Commercial. VTS in selected areas
12	156.600	156.600	Port Operations. VTS in selected areas
13	156.650	156.650	Intership Navigation Safety (Bridge-to-bridge). Ships >20m length maintain a listening watch on this channel in US waters

- Maritime VHF Channels utilize 5 kHz deviation wideband FM – 16K0F3E

* **NOTE** - In older VHF marine radios, simplex channels with a "A" suffix are the same channels in newer VHF marine radios with "10" channel prefix which to indicate simplex use of the ship station transmit frequency of an international duplex channel. Example "01A" is the same as "1001". Used in U.S. waters only.

Channel Number *	Ship Transmit MHz	Ship Receive MHz	Use
14	156.700	156.700	Port Operations. VTS in selected areas
15	–	156.750	Environmental (Receive only). Used by Class C EPIRBs
16	156.800	156.800	International Distress, Safety and Calling. Ships required to carry radio, USCG, and most coast stations maintain a listening watch on this channel
17	156.850	156.850	State & Local Government Maritime Control
18A	156.900	156.900	Commercial
19A	156.950	156.950	Commercial
20	157.000	161.600	Port Operations (duplex)
20A	157.000	157.000	Port Operations
21A	157.050	157.050	U.S. Coast Guard only
22A	157.100	157.100	Coast Guard Liaison and Maritime Safety Information Broadcasts. Broadcasts announced on Ch. 16
23A	157.150	157.150	U.S. Coast Guard only
24	157.200	161.800	Public Correspondence (Marine Operator)

- Maritime VHF Channels utilize 5 kHz deviation wideband FM – 16K0F3E

* **NOTE** - In older VHF marine radios, simplex channels with a "A" suffix are the same channels in newer VHF marine radios with "10" channel prefix which to indicate simplex use of the ship station transmit frequency of an international duplex channel. Example "22A" is the same as "1022". Used in U.S. waters only.

Channel Number *	Ship Transmit MHz	Ship Receive MHz	Use
25	157.250	161.850	Public Correspondence (Marine Operator)
26	157.300	161.900	Public Correspondence (Marine Operator)
27	157.350	161.950	Public Correspondence (Marine Operator)
28	157.400	162.000	Public Correspondence (Marine Operator)
63A*	156.175	156.175	Port Operations and Commercial, VTS. Available only in New Orleans/Lower Mississippi area.
65A*	156.275	156.275	Port Operations
66A*	156.325	156.325	Port Operations
67	156.375	156.375	Commercial. Used for bridge-to-bridge communications in lower Mississippi River. Intership only.
68	156.425	156.425	Non-Commercial
69	156.475	156.475	Non-Commercial
70	156.525	156.525	Digital Selective Calling (voice communications not allowed)
71	156.575	156.575	Non-Commercial

- Maritime VHF Channels utilize 5 kHz deviation wideband FM – 16K0F3E

* NOTE - In older VHF marine radios, simplex channels with a "A" suffix are the same channels in newer VHF marine radios with "10" channel prefix which to indicate simplex use of the ship station transmit frequency of an international duplex channel. Example "78A" is the same as "1078". Used in U.S. waters only.

Channel Number *	Ship Transmit MHz	Ship Receive MHz	Use
72	156.625	156.625	Non-Commercial (intership only)
73	156.675	156.675	Port Operations
74	156.725	156.725	Port Operations
77	156.875	156.875	Port Operations (intership only)
78A*	156.925	156.925	Non-Commercial
79A*	156.975	156.975	Commercial. Non-Commercial in Great Lakes only
80A*	157.025	157.025	Commercial. Non-Commercial in Great Lakes only
81A*	157.075	157.075	U.S. Government only - Environmental protection operations.
82A*	157.125	157.125	U.S. Government only
83A*	157.175	157.175	U.S. Coast Guard only
84	157.225	161.825	Public Correspondence (Marine Operator)
85	157.275	161.875	Public Correspondence (Marine Operator)
86	157.325	161.925	Public Correspondence (Marine Operator)

- Maritime VHF Channels utilize 5 kHz deviation wideband FM – 16K0F3E

* **NOTE** - In older VHF marine radios, simplex channels with a "A" suffix are the same channels in newer VHF marine radios with "10" channel prefix which to indicate simplex use of the ship station transmit frequency of an international duplex channel. Example "78A" is the same as "1078". Used in U.S. waters only.

Channel Number *	Ship Transmit MHz	Ship Receive MHz	Use
87	157.375	157.375	Public Correspondence (Marine Operator)
88	157.425	157.425	Commercial, Intership only.
AIS 1	161.975	161.975	Automatic Identification System (AIS)
AIS 2	162.025	162.025	Automatic Identification System (AIS)

- Maritime VHF Channels utilize 5 kHz deviation wideband FM – 16K0F3E

* **NOTE** - In older VHF marine radios, simplex channels with a "A" suffix are the same channels in newer VHF marine radios with "10" channel prefix which to indicate simplex use of the ship station transmit frequency of an international duplex channel. Example "78A" is the same as "1078". Used in U.S. waters only.

Shipboard repeaters:

457.525 457.550 457.575 457.600 MHz, wideband FM.

Inputs are +10.225 MHz

Foreign vessels may use +10.0 MHz offset outside U.S. waters.

On-board Communications:

Narrowband FM: 457.5375, 457.5625, 467.5375, 467.5625 MHz

Maritime Frequencies assignable to aircraft:

(HF) 2.738 2.830 3.023 4.125 5.680 MHz

(VHF) channels 6 8 9 16 1018 1022 67 68 72 & 88

See 47CFR §80.379 for restrictions.

Maritime Distress Frequencies - Radiotelephone:

(HF, USB - 2K80J3E) 2182, 4125*, 6215*, 8291*, 12290*, 16420 kHz

* Note – The USCG has proposed the termination of monitoring these voice frequencies in favor of Digital Selective Calling (DSC) distress messages; except for Kodiak, AK and Guam.

(VHF, FM wideband 5 kHz deviation - 16K0F3E) 156.800 MHz (Channel 16)

U.S. Coast Guard Rescue Coordination Centers		
24-hour Regional Contacts for Emergencies		
Last Modified 03/18/2021		
RCC	**Location**	**Phone Number**
Atlantic Area SAR Coordinator	Portsmouth, VA	(757) 398-6700
RCC Boston	Boston, MA	(617) 223-8555
RCC Norfolk	Portsmouth, VA	(757) 398-6231
RCC Miami	Miami, FL	(305) 415-6800
RSC San Juan*	San Juan, PR	(787) 289-2042
RCC New Orleans	New Orleans, LA	(504) 589-6225
RCC Cleveland	Cleveland, OH	(216) 902-6117
Pacific SAR Coordinator	Alameda, CA	(510) 437-3701
RCC Alameda	Alameda, CA	(510) 437-3701
RCC Seattle	Seattle, WA	(206) 220-7001
RCC Honolulu*	Honolulu, HI	(808) 535-3333
Sector Guam*	Santa Rita, GU	(671) 355-4824
RCC Juneau	Juneau, AK	(907) 463-2000

*NOTES:
- RSC San Juan is a Sub-Center of RCC Miami
- RCC Honolulu is operated as Joint RCC with DOD
- Sector Guam coordinates SAR under RCC Honolulu

Common Business Frequencies

LICENSING REQUIRED: Use of these channels must be licensed or authorized by STA.

IS = Special Industrial
IB = Industrial/Business

27.49	IB	Itinerant
35.04	IB	Itinerant
43.0400	IS	Itinerant
151.5050	IS	Itinerant
151.6250	IB	RED DOT Itinerant
151.9550	IB	**PURPLE DOT**
152.8700	IS	Itinerant
154.5700	IB	**BLUE DOT** (also MURS)
154.6000	IB	**GREEN DOT** (also MURS)
158.4000	IS	Itinerant
451.8000	IS	Itinerant
456.8000	IS	Itinerant
464.5000	IB	**BROWN DOT** Itinerant 35w.
464.5500	IB	**YELLOW DOT** Itinerant 35w.
467.7625	IB	**J DOT**
467.8125	IB	**K DOT**
467.8500	IB	**SILVER STAR**
467.8750	IB	**GOLD STAR**
467.9000	IB	**RED STAR**
467.9250	IB	**BLUE STAR**
469.5000	IB	Simplex or input to 464.500 if repeater. Itinerant 35 w. max
469.5500	IB	Simplex or input to 464.550 if repeater. Itinerant 35 w. max

Railroad Frequencies

160.2150(ch.007)-161.5650(ch.097), every 15 kHz
*Interstitial narrowband channels between Ch. 002-097 are offset 7.5 kHz.
161.2050 - Railroad Police Mutual Aid (channel 073)

Ch. 002-006 are used in Canada only:
(2) 159.8100   (4) 160.0500   (6) 160.2000
(3) 159.9300   (5) 160.1850

452.3250 / 457.3250
452.3750 / 457.3750
452.4250 / 457.4250
452.4750 / 457.4750

452.7750 / 457.7750
452.8250 / 457.8250
452.8750 / 452.8750
452.9000 / 457.9000

452.8500
452.8375 - low power
452.8625 - low power
452.8875 - low power

(*Telemetry/Remote Control/Remote Indicator frequencies
  omitted)
- Railroad police officers, as defined by the Federal Railroad
Administration (FRA) are allowed to operate on the FCC-designated
national interoperability channels with written concurrence from the
relevant state or state-designated interoperability coordinator and
are included in the blanket authorization for handheld and
vehicular-mounted radios. [See FCC R&O 16-113, released August
23, 2016]
- Many rail carriers have adopted NXDN modulation on some
  systems.

SAR (Search and Rescue) Frequencies

Land SAR

Typical frequencies are: 155.1600, .1750, .2050, .2200, .2350, .2650, .2800, or .2950

If CTCSS is required, try 127.3 Hz (3A).

LICENSING REQUIRED: Use of these channels must be licensed or authorized by STA. The FCC does not specify these as solely for SAR use, and these frequencies may be licensed locally for other uses. Monitor carefully before use.

Air SAR

3023, 5680, 8364 kHz upper sideband (lifeboat/survival craft),

4125 kHz upper sideband (distress/safety with ships and coast stations)

121.5 MHz emergency and distress

122.9 MHz SAR secondary & training

123.1 MHz SAR primary

Water SAR

156.3000 (VHF Marine Ch. 06) Safety and SAR

156.4500 (VHF Marine Ch. 09) Non-commercial supplementary calling

156.8000 (VHF Marine Ch. 16) DISTRESS and calling

156.8500 (VHF Marine Ch. 17) State & Local Government Maritime Control

157.1000 (VHF Marine Ch. 22A) Coast Guard Liaison

VHF Marine Channels

6, 9, 15, 16, 21A, 22A (USCG Liaison), 23A, 81A, 83A

USCG Auxiliary

138.4750, 142.8250, 143.4750, 149.2000, 150.7000

USCG/DOD Joint SAR

345.0 MHz AM initial contact, 282.8 MHz AM working

Military SAR

40.5000 wideband FM	US Army/USN SAR
138.450 AM, 138.750 AM	USAF SAR

Standard Time and Frequency Broadcasts

Radio station WWV (Fort Collins, Colorado), WWVH (Kauai, Hawaii), and CHU (Ontario, Canada) broadcast continuous time signals on precise frequencies. Because the broadcasts occur simultaneously on several HF frequencies at high power, at least one of the signals should be receivable at all times throughout the US and Canada. This can be useful for testing HF receivers and antennas, and for selecting frequencies based on currently observable propagation.

Frequencies (MHz)		
WWV*	WWVH*	CHU
2.500	2.500	3.330
5.000	5.000	7.850
10.000	10.000	14.670
15.000	15.000	
20.000		
25.000		
Double Sideband AM	Double Sideband AM	Full Carrier USB
Male Voice	Female Voice	English and French

*WWV broadcasts Military Auxiliary Radio System (MARS) announcements on the 10th minute of each hour, and WWVH on the 50th minute.

Standard Time by Telephone

1-303-499-7111 - WWV (Colorado) 1-808-335-4363 - WWVH (Hawaii)

1-202-762-1401, 1-202-762-1069 (DSN 762-1401, 762-1069) - Washington, DC

1-719-567-6742 (DSN 560-6742) - Colorado Springs, CO

The Washington DC and Colorado Springs CO lines alternate between local (EST/EDT or MST/MDT) and UTC (Z) time.

HF Disaster Communications

Fixed, Base, Mobile		Fixed	
2326	I	5135	A
2411		5140	A, I
2414		5192	I
2419		5195	I
2422		7477	A
2439		7480	A
2463		7802	D
2466		7805	I
2471		7932	
2474		7935	C, D
2487			
2511			
2535			
2569			
2587			
2801			
2804	A		
2812			

- Carrier frequencies in kHz. A=Alternate channel I=Interstate coordination C=Conterminous US D=Daytime Operations Only
- **May be licensed only to the central governments of the 50 states and 6 US territories.** See FCC rules 90.264, 90.20(d)(6), and 90.129(m).
- Emissions: Only 2K80J3E (USB), 100HA1A and those emission types listed in §90.237(g) are permitted.
- Capability is often referred to as "Operations SECURE", for State Emergency Communications Using Radio Effectively

HF Long Distance Communications

Fixed, Base, Mobile		Fixed (including itinerant)			
2289		5046.6	E	7480.1	
2292		5052.6	E	7483.1	
2395		5055.6	E	7486.1	E
2398		5061.6	W	7549.1	D
3170		5067.6		7552.1	
4538.6	N	5074.6	E	7555.1	W
4548.6	N	5099.1		7558.1	W
4575		5102.1		7559.1	W
4610.5		5313.6		7562.1	W
4613.5				7697.1	
4634.5		6800.1	N		
4637.5		6803.1			
4647		6806.1	W		
		6855.1	N,M		
		6858.1	N		
		6861.1	W		
		6885.1	N		
		6888.1	N		

- Carrier frequencies in kHz.
- **D** = Daytime Operations Only, **N** = Night Operations Only, **E** = East of 108° West Longitude (WL), **M** = West of the Mississippi River, **W** = West of 90° WL.
- **May be licensed for repair of telecommunications circuits, power & pipeline distribution etc.** See FCC rules 90.266, 90.35(c)(1), and 90.129(o).
- Emissions: Only 2K80J3E (USB), 100HA1A, 100HA1B, and those emission types listed in §90.237(g) are permitted.

Maritime HF and VHF Distress Frequencies

Global Maritime Distress & Safety System, Digital Selective Calling (DSC) & Radiotelephone Channels - **for use only by vessels and coast stations authorized in the Maritime Services** (FCC Part 80, NTIA 7.5 and 8.2.29). These are **not** nationwide interoperability channels and are **not** for land-based public safety agencies. *These frequencies may be programmed only into radios certificated for Part 80 operations, and only by a person holding a First or Second Class Radiotelegraph Operator's Certificate, Radiotelegraph Operator License, or General Radiotelephone Operator License.*

The simplex DSC frequencies except 2187.5 and 16804.5 kHz are monitored by the US Coast Guard and are used for digital alerting and calling for distress, urgency and safety. Once the DSC call has been sent, the corresponding radiotelephone frequency is used for voice communications.

The simplex voice frequencies are used for distress and safety communications, and except for 2182 and 16420 kHz are monitored by the USCG. Frequencies are monitored according to propagation; not all frequencies are monitored at all times. These radiotelephone channels use upper sideband (USB - 2K80J3E); the frequency shown is the suppressed carrier reference frequency. VHF channel 16 uses wideband FM (16K0F3E or 16K0G3E).

DSC	Voice
2187.5 kHz	2182 kHz*
4207.5 kHz	4125 kHz
6312.0 kHz	6215 kHz
8414.5 kHz	8291 kHz
12577.0 kHz	12290 kHz
16804.5 kHz	16420 kHz*
156.5250 MHz (Channel 70)	156.8000 MHz (channel 16)
* International distress channel that is not monitored by USCG The USCG has proposed the termination of monitoring these voice frequencies in favor of Digital Selective Calling (DSC) distress messages; except in Kodiak, AK and Guam.	

SHARES HF

SHARES is the SHAred RESources HF Radio Program operated by CISA.

Interoperability, backup emergency communications, and situational awareness are the main uses. Operations include nationwide and regional radio nets for voice and data communications, and there is a nationwide HF email network that operates with or without the conventional internet, fully automatically. All SHARES HF channels are authorized for use throughout the U.S. and Possessions.

Access to the SHARES networks requires registration with the SHARES Program Office. Government agencies of federal, state, county, and major cities are eligible, as are operators of critical infrastructure and key resources, and national or regional (multi-state) disaster relief organizations.

SHARES is a government radio network. It is not amateur radio, and registration is not open to amateur radio operators (hams).

Do not wait for an emergency to try to arrange access to SHARES. Learn about the program now at cisa.gov/shares and if you are interested and eligible, contact the SHARES Program office via shares@cisa.dhs.gov or +1-703-235-5329.

Alaska Emergency Frequency

5167.5 kHz USB carrier frequency, 5168.9 kHz assigned (center) frequency

Any stations authorized in the maritime, private land mobile, and amateur parts of the FCC rules, and federal government stations authorized by NTIA rules, are allowed to communicate with any other duly authorized station in the State of Alaska for emergency communications provided that all stations operating on this frequency must be located in or within 50 nautical miles (92.6 km) of the State of Alaska. Maximum power permitted is 150W Peak Envelop Power (PEP). [47 CFR §80.387, §90.253, §97.401, NTIA Manual §7.3.8(3)]

A (amateur) station in, or within 92.6 km of, Alaska may transmit communications for tests and training drills necessary to ensure the establishment, operation, and maintenance of emergency communication systems. [47 CFR §97.401]

Amateur Radio Emergency Frequencies

These frequencies are not available for licensing to Public Safety agencies. A valid Amateur Radio Operator License of the appropriate class is required in order to transmit on these frequencies.

Emergency Center of Activity Frequencies - emergency communications networks in North/Central/South America and the Caribbean are encouraged to establish their operations within 20 kHz +/- of these frequencies (kHz):

3750 or 3985 LSB	7060, 7240, or 7290 LSB	
14300 USB	18160 USB	21360 USB

60-meter Band (5 MHz)

The intended use for these five channels is interoperability between federal government stations and licensed U.S. amateur radio stations. Federal government stations are Primary users and amateurs are Secondary users. DHS (including FEMA) and USCG stations, among others, have existing frequency authorizations aligned with the five Amateur Service secondary channels at 5 MHz and have priority for radio traffic. In an emergency, or a test coordinated by FEMA, these five channels may be used between federal government stations and licensed U.S. General, Advanced, or Extra class amateur radio stations in coordination with the FCC and NTIA.

Permitted operating modes include upper sideband voice (USB), CW, RTTY, PSK31 and other digital modes such as PACTOR III. Only one signal at a time is permitted on any channel.

Carrier Frequency (kHz)	Center Frequency (kHz)
5330.5	5332.0
5346.5	5348.0
5357.0	5358.5
5371.5	5373.0
5403.5	5405.0

Amateur Radio Emergency Frequencies

Automatic Link Establishment (ALE) hflink.com/channels/
Emergency/Disaster Relief Interoperation Voice Channels (kHz, USB*):

Netcall: HFL	
1996.0	10131.0
3996.0	14346.0
5357.0	18117.5
5371.5	21432.5
7296.0	28312.5

Text Message Channels (kHz, USB*):

Netcall: HFN	
1843.0	18106.0
3596.0	21096.0
7102.0	24926.0
10145.5	28146.0
14109.0	

* Carrier reference frequency (center of ALE signal is offset +1625 Hz)

Maritime Mobile Service Net (and others): 14300 kHz USB mmsn.org

Hurricane Watch Net: 14325 kHz USB hwn.org

National Hurricane Center, during hurricanes (kHz):

14325 USB - Day		7268 LSB - Night	
3815 LSB - Caribbean	3950 LSB - North Florida	3940 LSB - South Florida

IRLP Node: 9219, Alternate Node: 9508 or 9123

EchoLink Conference: "WX-TALK" Node 7203

EchoLink Alternate Conference: "VKEMCOMM"

w4ehw.fiu.edu/wx4nhc-contact.html

Amateur Radio Calling Frequencies

Band	Frequency (MHz)	Mode
80 Meters	3.885	AM
40 Meters	7.290	AM
20 Meters	14.286	AM
6 Meters	50.125	SSB
6 Meters	52.525	FM Simplex
6 Meters	52.540	FM Simplex
6 Meters	50.620	Digital (packet)
2 Meters	144.200	SSB
2 Meters	146.520	FM Simplex
1.25 Meters	222.100	CW/SSB
70 Centimeters	432.100	CW/SSB
70 Centimeters	446.000	FM Simplex
33 Centimeters	902.100	CW/SSB
33 Centimeters	903.100	CW/SSB
33 Centimeters	927.500	FM Simplex
23 Centimeters	1294.500	FM Simplex
23 Centimeters	1296.100	CW/SSB

These frequencies are not available for licensing to Public Safety agencies. A valid Amateur Radio Operator License of the appropriate class is required in order to transmit on these frequencies.

FM amateur calling frequencies use carrier squelch. A mixture of digital modes or mixed modes could be found locally (P25, NDXN, DMR, etc.)

Amateur Radio Repeater Coordinators

arrl.org/files/file/Coordinators/Participating%20Coordinators.pdf

Amateur Radio Bands (US)

Amateurs wishing to operate on either 2,200 or 630 meters must first register with the Utilities Technology Council online at
https://utc.org/plc-database-amateur-notification-process/
You need only register once for each band.

License Classes
E = Amateur Extra   A = Advanced
G = General   T = Technician   N = Novice

2,200 Meters (135 kHz)

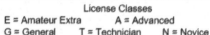

135.7 kHz   1 W EIRP maximum   **137.8 kHz**

E,A,G

630 Meters (472 kHz)

5 W EIRP maximum, except in Alaska within 496 miles of Russia where the power limit is 1 W EIRP.

E,A,G

472 kHz   **479 kHz**

160 Meters (1.8 MHz)

Avoid interference to radiolocation operations from 1.900 to 2.000 MHz

E,A,G

1.800   1.900   2.000 MHz

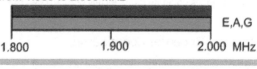

RTTY & data   Phone & Image   CW only

Amateur Radio Bands (US) - continued

80 Meters (3.5 MHz)

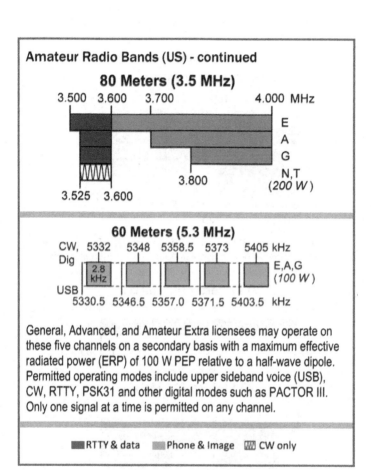

60 Meters (5.3 MHz)

General, Advanced, and Amateur Extra licensees may operate on these five channels on a secondary basis with a maximum effective radiated power (ERP) of 100 W PEP relative to a half-wave dipole. Permitted operating modes include upper sideband voice (USB), CW, RTTY, PSK31 and other digital modes such as PACTOR III. Only one signal at a time is permitted on any channel.

■■■RTTY & data   ■■■Phone & Image   ▨▨ CW only

Amateur Radio Bands (US) – continued
40 Meters (7 MHz)

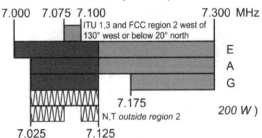

7.000 7.075 7.100   7.300 MHz

ITU 1,3 and FCC region 2 west of
130° west or below 20° north

E
A
G

7.175
N,T *outside region 2*   *200 W*)

7.025   7.125

See Sections 97.305(c), 97.307(f)(11) and 97.301(e). These exemptions do not apply to stations in the continental US.

30 Meters (10.1 MHz)
Avoid interference to fixed services outside the US.

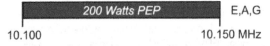

200 Watts PEP   E,A,G

10.100   10.150 MHz

20 Meters (14 MHz)

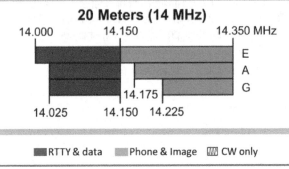

14.000   14.150   14.350 MHz

E
A
G

14.175

14.025   14.150   14.225

■RTTY & data   ■Phone & Image   ▨ CW only

Amateur Radio Bands (US) – continued

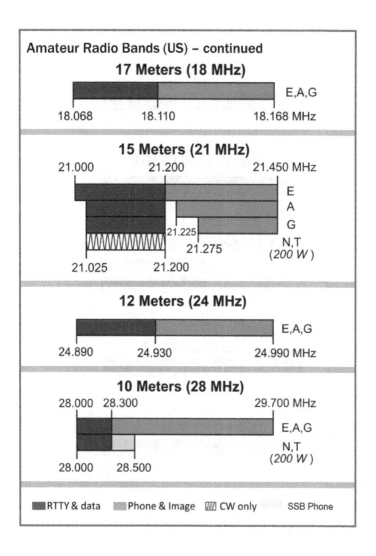

17 Meters (18 MHz)

E,A,G

18.068   18.110   18.168 MHz

15 Meters (21 MHz)

21.000   21.200   21.450 MHz

E

A

G

N,T
(*200 W*)

21.225

21.275

21.025   21.200

12 Meters (24 MHz)

E,A,G

24.890   24.930   24.990 MHz

10 Meters (28 MHz)

28.000 28.300   29.700 MHz

E,A,G

N,T
(*200 W*)

28.000   28.500

■ RTTY & data   ■ Phone & Image   ▧ CW only   SSB Phone

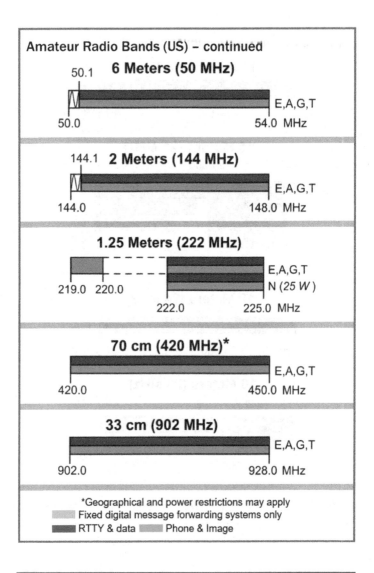

Amateur Radio Bands (US) – continued

6 Meters (50 MHz)

50.1
50.0
54.0 MHz
E,A,G,T

2 Meters (144 MHz)

144.1
144.0
148.0 MHz
E,A,G,T

1.25 Meters (222 MHz)

219.0 220.0
222.0
225.0 MHz
E,A,G,T
N (*25 W*)

70 cm (420 MHz)*

420.0
450.0 MHz
E,A,G,T

33 cm (902 MHz)

902.0
928.0 MHz
E,A,G,T

*Geographical and power restrictions may apply
Fixed digital message forwarding systems only
RTTY & data   Phone & Image

Amateur Radio Bands (US) – continued

23 cm (1240 MHz)*

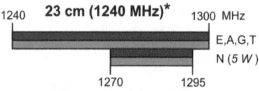

1240   1300 MHz

E,A,G,T

N (*5 W*)

1270   1295

Automatically Controlled Digital Stations.

A station may be automatically controlled while transmitting a RTTY or data emission on the 6 m or shorter wavelength bands, and on the 28.120-28.189 MHz, 24.925-24.930 MHz, 21.090-21.100 MHz, 18.105-18.110 MHz, 14.0950-14.0995 MHz, 14.1005-14.112 MHz, 10.140-10.150 MHz, 7.100-7.105 MHz, or 3.585-3.600 MHz segments provided that:

(1) The station is responding to interrogation by a station under local or remote control; and

(2) No transmission from the automatically controlled station occupies a bandwidth of more than 500 Hz.

This rule section does not apply to an auxiliary station, a beacon station, a repeater station, an earth station, a space station, or a space telecommand station.

(FCC rule 97.221)

Automatically controlled digital stations may operate on all authorized frequencies above 50.1 MHz when the control operator is present at the control point, in which case the 500 Hz bandwidth limitation does not apply.

Amateur Radio Bands (US) – continued

All licensees except Novice are authorized all modes
on the following frequencies:

2300-2310 MHz	47.0-47.2 GHz
2390-2450 MHz	76.0-81.0 GHz
3300-3500 MHz	122.25-123.0 GHz
5650-5925 MHz	134-141 GHz
10.0-10.5 GHz	241-250 GHz
24.0-24.25 GHz	All above 275 GHz

Amateur Radio Power Limits (US)

FCC Rule 47 CFR §97.313

(a) An amateur station must use the minimum transmitter power necessary to carry out the desired communications.

(b) No station may transmit with a transmitter power exceeding 1.5 kW PEP.

[60 meters: 100W PEP ERP; 30 meters: 200W PEP; additional restrictions apply under certain conditions, and to Novice and Technician licensees.]

Personal Radio Services

Multi-Use Radio Service (MURS) Channels

License Not Required for Operations
Strictly Prohibited for use by the NMAC on Wildfire Incidents

CH	Frequency (MHz)	CH	Frequency (MHz)	CH	Frequency (MHz)
1	151.8200	2	151.8800	3	151.9400
4*	154.5700	5*	154.6000		
		2 Watts Max			

- MURS equipment must be certified per FCC Rules, 47 CFR Parts 2 and 95 Subpart J (47 CFR §95.2761)
- MURS frequencies are not authorized to transmit in Part 90 certified equipment.
- Authorized emission types: A1D, A2B, A2D, A3E, F2B, F1D, F2D, F3E, G3E
- Authorized bandwidth: 11.25 kHz (151.8200, 151.8800, & 151.9400) 20 kHz (154.5700 & 154.6000)
- External gain antennas may be used (must be no more than 60 feet above ground, or 20 feet above the structure on which it is mounted.
- Voice or data, except:
No store-and-forward packet operation
No continuous carrier operation
No interconnection with the public switched network
No use aboard aircraft in flight
* Frequencies are shared with itinerant Industrial-Business operations.

Citizens Band (CB) Channels & Frequencies

License Not Required for Operations

CH	Frequency	CH	Frequency	CH	Frequency	CH	Frequency
1	26.9650	11	27.0850	21	27.2150	31	27.3150
2	26.9750	12	27.1050	22	27.2250	32	27.3250
3	26.9850	13	27.1150	23*	27.2550	33	27.3350
4	27.0050	14	27.1250	24	27.2350	34	27.3450
5	27.0150	15	27.1350	25	27.2450	35	27.3550
6	27.0250	16	27.1550	26	27.2650	36	27.3650
7	27.0350	17	27.1650	27	27.2750	37	27.3750
8	27.0550	18	27.1750	28	27.2850	38	27.3850
9	27.0650	19	27.1850	29	27.2950	39	27.3950
10	27.0750	20	27.2050	30	27.3050	40	27.4050

- CB equipment must be certified per FCC Rules, 47 CFR Parts 2 and 95, Subpart D (47 CFR §95.961)
- Amplitude Modulated (AM) voice signals, the mean carrier power must not exceed 4 Watts. (47 CFR §95.967)
- Single Sideband (SSB) voice signals; peak envelope power must not exceed 12 Watts
- Authorized emission types: A3E, J3E, R3E, and H3E (47 CFR §95.971)
*Shared with the Remote Control Radio Service (RCRS), 47 CFR Part 95, Subpart C.
Other RCRS frequencies close to CB include: 26.9950, 27.0450, 27.0950, 27.1450, and 27.1950 MHz

Family Radio Service (FRS) Channels

License Not Required for Operations

Strictly Prohibited for use by NMAC on Wildfire Incidents

CH	Frequency	CH	Frequency	CH	Frequency
1	462.5625	8	467.5625	15	462.5500
2	462.5875	9	467.5875	16	462.5750
3	462.6125	10	467.6125	17	462.6000
4	462.6375	11	467.6375	18	462.6250
5	462.6625	12	467.6625	19	462.6500
6	462.6875	13	467.6875	20	462.6750
7	462.7125	14	467.7125	21	462.7000
				22	462.7250
2 watts ERP Max		**0.5 watts ERP Max**		**2 watts ERP Max**	

- FRS frequencies are not authorized to transmit in Part 90 certified equipment.
- FRS equipment must be certified per FCC Rules, 47 CFR Part 95, Subparts B and J (47 CFR §95.561)
- FRS shares the same simplex frequencies as GMRS. (47 CFR §95.563)
- Authorized emission types: F2D, G2D, F3E, G3E (47 CFR §95.571)
- Authorized bandwidth: 12.5 kHz (47 CFR §95.573)

General Mobile Radio Service (GMRS) Channels & Frequencies

Personal Use Only - License Required for Operations

Strictly Prohibited for use by NMAC on Wildfire Incidents

Interstitial Channels					Main Channels		
5 watts ERP Max		0.5 watts ERP Max*			50 Watts Max		
CH	Frequency	CH	Frequency	CH	Frequency	Repeater Input Frequency	
1	462.5625	8	467.5625	15	462.5500	467.5500	
2	462.5875	9	467.5875	16	462.5750	467.5750	
3	462.6125	10	467.6125	17	462.6000	467.6000	
4	462.6375	11	467.6375	18	462.6250	467.6250	
5	462.6625	12	467.6625	19	462.6500	467.6500	
6	462.6875	13	467.6875	20*	462.6750	467.6750	
7	462.7125	14	467.7125	21	462.7000	467.7000	
		* Handheld Only		22	462.7250	467.7250	

- GMRS frequencies are not authorized to transmit in Part 90 certified equipment.
- GMRS equipment must be certified per FCC Rules, 47 CFR Part 95, Subpart E (47 CFR §95.1761)
- GMRS shares the simplex frequencies for labeled as FRS, channels 1-22.
- Authorized bandwidth: 20 kHz for 462 MHz interstitial and 462/467 MHz Main Channels (47 CFR §95.1773)
- North of Line A / East of Line C: 462.6500, 467.6500, 462.7000, 467.7000 may not be used; small control stations limited to 5 Watts. *Nationwide Travel's assistance; if CTCSS is required try 141.3 Hz.

Interference Management

Radio Frequency (RF) Interference

Normal day-to-day operations, special events, and even in emergency and disaster situations, could all be subject to RF Interference at some point. Timely, proper identification and mitigation of any potential interference issues is critical to minimize any interruption of mission-critical communications.

Several symptoms of RF interference may include disruption or failure of wireless communications or equipment for unknown reasons such as:

- Cannot communicate in areas where they typically have radio or cell coverage;
- Cannot communicate with normally reliable base radios or repeaters;
- Cannot communicate on multiple communications devices using multiple bands;
- Notice a significant loss of functionality or general failure of GPS systems;

Realize communications improve significantly when moving a short distance away from a specific fixed area, or "dead zone."

There are three main categories of RF interference that can affect mission - critical public safety communications:

- Internal or Self Interference
- External Interference
- Intentional Interference (also known as Electronic Jamming)

Internal or Self Interference

Internal or self-interference is a type of unintentional RF interference which occurs when an organization's own devices may be operating in a manner that interferes with their internal communications. These could be cause by:

- Equipment Problems
- Receiver Intermodulation
- Incorrect Setup
- Front-End Overload

External Interference

External interference is a type of unintentional RF interference that can result from sources like those associated with internal RF interference but exist outside of an organization's jurisdiction or control. Four types of External RF Interference are:

- Co-Channel
- Adjacent Channel
- Spurious Emissions
- Natural Occurrences

Intentional Interference (Jamming)

Intentional interference – or jamming – is performed by an actor with a willful intent to disrupt, disconnect, or degrade communications. Malicious jamming and nuisance jamming are the two types of intentional interference. Malicious jamming is conducted by individuals with willful and criminal intent. The criminal intent may be to prevent public safety personnel from completing their mission, or conceal an ongoing criminal activity, among other possible motivations.

RF Interference Mitigation

The RF interference mitigation cycle includes five steps: Recognize, Respond, Report, Resolve, and Resilience. Employ these steps continuously in order to robustly defend against RF interference.

Initial steps can be taken to mitigate, as well as identify potential RF Interference such as:

Figure 3: RF Interference Mitigation Lifecycle

- Alert the communications team, commander, and dispatch
- Attempt rotating the radio antenna element 90°, so the antenna is horizontal to the terrain
- Switch to tactical channels
- Switch to a different means of communication, preferably on a different band (e.g., switching from cellular to UHF or VHF bands or Satellite Communications [SATCOM] could be a potential course of action)
- Shield the mobile radio behind a wall or large vehicle
- Find higher ground.
- If possible, turn on the automatic gain control on your radio.
- Report the incident to the Incident Communications Center and the COML
- Report and coordinate interference incidents with your Statewide Interoperability Coordinator (SWIC)
- Consider sharing the information with neighboring jurisdictions

RF Interference Mitigation - continued

After performing local mitigations, it is important for officials to report RF interference to the appropriate national-level authorities. Those reporting should be prepared to provide as many details as possible on the incident, including:

- Start a dedicated log to document information, including time the interference start and stops, etc.
- Complaining party's name, contact information, agency, date, time, duration, location, and affected mission or operations;
- Nature of the disruption (e.g., single occurrence, recurring, intermittent, or loss of signal indication), the affected equipment (e.g., type, model, application) and any devices that continue to function properly;
- "What does it sound like?"
- Recordings, spectrum analyzer screenshots, and incident logs with location tagging;
- Environmental conditions (e.g., weather, topography, terrain, time of day);
- Steps taken to improve or regain ability to use equipment; and
- Possible cause of the disruption, information on the suspected interfering/jamming device, and details on the suspected operator of the illegal equipment (e.g., name, date of birth, vehicle tag).

Authority	Contact Information
FCC 24/7 Operations Center	fcc.gov/general/public-safety-support-center Complaint Form: fccprod.servicenowservices.com/psix-esix?id=psix_form (202) 418-1122 FCCOPS@fcc.gov
Non-Aviation GPS Outages: USCG	navcen.uscg.gov/?pageName=gpsUserInput
Aviation GPS Outages: FAA	faa.gov/air_traffic/nas/gps_reports/
Military GPS Outages worldwide: GPSOC	gps.afspc.af.mil/ (may not open for non-military users)

USEFUL REFERENCES

Operations Center Telephone Numbers

DHS	Main Number	202-282-8000
	NOC Senior Watch Officer	202-282-8101
CISA	NCC Watch	703-235-5080
	SHARES HF Radio	703-235-5329
	SHARES Email: shares@cisa.dhs.gov	
	CISA Central Email: central@cisa.dhs.gov	
FCC	FCC Operations Center (FCCOC)	202-418-1122, - 2813 FAX
	FCC Email FCCOPS@fcc.gov / FCCOPcenter@fcc.gov	
	General Info (1-888-CALL-FCC)	1-888-225-5322, 1-866-418-0232 FAX
FEMA	National Watch Center	202-646-2828
	National Response Coordination Center (NRCC)	202-212-2424
	NRCC Email FEMA-NRCC@fema.dhs.gov	
FPS	Federal Protective Service, National Emergency Number	1-877-4FPS-411 (437-7411)
ARC	American National Red Cross	
	24-hr Disaster Operations Center	800-526-3571, 202-303-5555
	American Radio Relay League Email emergency@arrl.org	
ARRL	Main Number	860-594-0200, - 0259 FAX
	Emergency Preparedness Manager	860-594-0222
	Radio Station W1AW	860-594-0268

National Council of Statewide Interoperability Coordinators (NCSWIC) Membership: cisa.gov/safecom/ncswic-membership

SAFECOM: cisa.gov/safecom

CISA Emergency Communications (CISA): cisa.gov/emergency-communications

Electronic Code of Federal Regulations – Title 47 Telecommunication: ecfr.gov

FCC Universal Licensing System (ULS): fcc.gov/uls

National Public Safety Telecommunications Council (NPSTC): npstc.org

National Regional Planning Council (NRPC): nrpc.us

NTIA Red Book: ntia.doc.gov/page/2011/manual-regulations-and-procedures-federal-radio-frequency-management-redbook

CISA/FEMA Regions - States and Territories

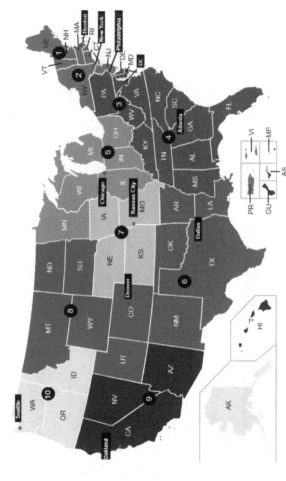

Figure 4: CISA/FEMA Regions- States and Territories

CISA Region Contacts

CISA Central | central@cisa.dhs.gov | 888-282-0870

CISA Regions	Email
Region 1: CT, MA, ME, NH, RI, VT	CISARegion1@hq.dhs.gov
Region 2: NJ, NY, Puerto Rico (PR) and United States Virgin Islands (USVI)	CISARegion2@hq.dhs.gov
Region 3: DC, DE, MD, PA, VA, WV	CISARegion3@hq.dhs.gov
Region 4: AL, FL, GA, KY, MS, NC, SC, TN	CISARegion4@hq.dhs.gov
Region 5: IL, IN, MI, MN, OH, WI	CISARegion5@hq.dhs.gov
Region 6: AR, LA, NM, OK, TX	CISARegion6@hq.dhs.gov
Region 7: IA, KS, MO, NE	CISARegion7@hq.dhs.gov
Region 8: CO, MT, ND, SD, UT, WY	CISARegion8@hq.dhs.gov
Region 9: AZ, CA, Guam (GU), HI, NV, Commonwealth of the Northern Mariana Islands (CNMI), Republic of the Marshall Islands (RMI), Federated States of Micronesia (FSM), American Samoa (AS)	CISARegion9@hq.dhs.gov
Region 10: AK, ID, OR, WA	CISARegion10@hq.dhs.gov

FEMA Region Contacts

FEMA Regions | FEMA.gov **FEMA HQ, Washington DC:** 1-202-646-2500 **FEMA Disaster Assistance:** 1-800-621-FEMA (3362)

FEMA Regions	FEMA Contact Number
Region 1: CT, MA, ME, NH, RI, VT	1-617-956-7506 or 1-877-336-2734
Region 2: NJ, NY, Puerto Rico (PR) and United States Virgin Islands (USVI)	NJ and NY: 1-212-680-3600 PR and USVI: 1-787-296-3500
Region 3: DC, DE, MD, PA, VA, WV	1-215-931-5500
Region 4: AL, FL, GA, KY, MS, NC, SC, TN	1-770-220-5200
Region 5: IL, IN, MI, MN, OH, WI	1-312-408-5500
Region 6: AR, LA, NM, OK, TX	1-940-898-5399
Region 7: IA, KS, MO, NE	1-816-283-7061
Region 8: CO, MT, ND, SD, UT, WY	1-303-235-4800
Region 9: AZ, CA, Guam (GU), HI, NV, Commonwealth of the Northern Mariana Islands (CNMI), Republic of the Marshall Islands (RMI), Federated States of Micronesia (FSM), American Samoa (AS)	1-510-627-7100
Region 10: AK, ID, OR, WA	1-425-487-4600

Emergency Support Functions (ESF)

ESF #1	Transportation
ESF #2	Communications
ESF #3	Public Works and Engineering
ESF #4	Firefighting
ESF #5	Information and Planning
ESF #6	Mass Care, Emergency Assistance, Temporary Housing, and Human Services
ESF #7	Logistics
ESF #8	Public Health and Medical Services
ESF #9	Search and Rescue
ESF #10	Oil and Hazardous Materials Response
ESF #11	Agriculture and Natural Resources Annex
ESF #12	Energy
ESF #13	Public Safety and Security
ESF #14	Cross-Sector Business and Infrastructure
ESF #15	External Affairs

Priority Telecommunications Services (PTS) Programs

For assistance and information on all CISA Priority Telecommunications
Services programs, contact the Priority Telecommunications Service Center at
1-866-627-2255, 703-676-2255, or support@priority-info.com

GETS – Govt. Emergency Telecommunications Service

cisa.gov/gets

(see next page for GETS access info)

WPS – Wireless Priority Service

cisa.gov/wps

(see next page for WPS access info)

GETS and WPS provide priority on voice networks.

TSP – Telecommunications Service Priority

cisa.gov/tsp

For restoration priority on circuits that have been enrolled in the TSP program,
place a trouble ticket with the service provider; reminding of the TSP designation
and providing the TSP authorization codes for the affected circuits. TSP
restoration priority is available only for circuits that have been enrolled in the
TSP program before the outage occurred.

For TSP provisioning priority (installation of a new circuit), contact the CISA
Priority Telecommunications Service Center at 1-866-627-2255, 703-676-2255,
or support@priority-info.com.

PTS Dialer

The "PTS Dialer" app provides a streamlined way of making priority calls. To
download the PTS Dialer App, visit gets-wps.csgov.com/apps.

Government Emergency Telecommunications Service Card

Government Emergency Telecommunications Service

John Smith
State of Montana Highway Patrol

Dial Access Number: **1-710-627-4387**

After Tone, Enter PIN: ************

When Prompted, Dial: **Area Code + Number**

GETS

If your 1-710-627-4387 call fails,
try an alternate access number

1-888-288-4387	**AT&T**
1-877-646-4387	**AT&T**
1-855-333-4387▲	**Sprint**
1-800-900-4387▲	**Verizon**
1-855-400-4387▲	**Verizon**

▲ *Use for GETS calls to toll-free destination numbers*

WIRELESS PRIORITY SERVICE

*272 + Area Code + Number + SEND

From a WPS-Enabled Phone

www.cisa.gov/gets | www.cisa.gov/wps
Warning: For Official Use Only by Authorized Personnel

24 Hour Assistance

Help/trouble reporting

1-800-818-4387
or **703-818-4387**

Familiarization Calls

*Make periodic GETS
and WPS test calls to*

703-818-3924

U.S. Government Property

If found, return to:
DHS/CISA
245 Murray Lane SW
Mail Stop 0613
Washington, DC 20528

Figure 5: Government Emergency Telecommunications Service Card

EMERGENCY WIRELESS CARRIER SERVICES

Not every incident requires deploying full a site on wheels. A trailer, tethered drone, or network optimization may address your requirements. If you believe your incident or planned event will require additional coverage or capacity, reach out to the wireless carrier.

In a large incident, you may request the State EOC ESF-2 desk to assist with your request for coverage enhancements or deployment of additional handsets/hotspot devices.

For planned events or demonstration equipment, you should submit your request well in advance, typically 30 days or more.

Typical Information Required for Requesting Deployable Cellular Infrastructure:

- What are the communications needs?
- What issues or problems are you facing?
- Where is the coverage needed? Number of users and/or devices?
- What will the devices be doing?
- What are the incident conditions, including environmental concerns and size of incident?
- What is terrain and access?
- Is the roadway accessible?
- Height/weight restrictions, turning radius adequate?
- Will there be an escort required?
- Where is the desired site setup?
- Site secure?
- Level clear area with 100' x 100' minimum space with southern view?

Typical Customer Support Request Information

Short Summary of situation:

Incident Name:

Requesting Agency Name:

Support Location Address or Lat/Long:

Start Date:

End Date:

Location POC Name:

Location POC Phone:

Location POC email (If available):

Do you need Data:

- Connection Type
  - Wired:
  - WiFi:
  - Indoor Coverage:

    Approx. Sq ft.:

  - Outdoor Coverage:

    Approximate Square ft.:

- Approximately how many end users need support:
  - Quantity Indoor
  - Quantity Outdoor

Power availability: Commercial or Generator

Do you need cellular coverage?

Do you need devices:

Quantity and Type:

FirstNet Response Operations Group (ROG)

24/7/365 FirstNet Help Desk: 800-574-7000
firstnet.com
Foundation Account Number (FAN) will be needed for support.

The FirstNet mission is to deploy, operate, maintain, and improve the only high-speed, nationwide wireless broadband network dedicated to public safety. FirstNet is a constantly expanding and evolving network with investments focused on meeting current and future mission-critical requirements of public safety.

Background - The First Responder Network Authority has entered a 25-year public-private partnership with AT&T. AT&T brings a proven track record and strong commitment to public safety, as well as the commercial expertise and nationwide resources to deploy, maintain and operate the network.

Services Offered:

- Agencies subscribing to FirstNet services can request deployable support 24/7 for disasters, critical incidents, and planned events.

- Provided at no cost to FirstNet subscriber agencies, including associated support costs (fuel, personnel, satellite airtime).

- More than 100 assets dedicated to FirstNet users, built with 4G LTE solutions, which are strategic distributed throughout the United States:

  - Satellite-connected Cells on Light Trucks (SatCOLTs)
  - Satellite Cells on Wheels (SatCOWs)
  - Emergency Communications Vehicles
  - FirstNet One (aerostat)
  - Compact Rapid Deployables (CRDs)
  - Mobile Deployment Kits
  - Cel-Fi Go Red Kits (FirstNet Cellular Signal Booster)

How do FirstNet Deployables work?

- Can provide several miles of coverage (dependent upon site conditions and terrain)

- Typically, radiates Band 14 for best public safety experience

- Locked to the FirstNet Black SIM card

- SatCOLTs and SatCOWs establish backhaul via satellite

- Provide voice (including Voice over IP, VoLTE), data, location, and messaging

- 14-hour window for arrival and operational status for emergent incident responses

- 30-day notice required for planned events

- Deployables are intended to support FirstNet users with FirstNet capable devices - not consumer cellular traffic

How do you request a FirstNet deployable?

- Call the 24/7/365 FirstNet Help Desk: 800-574-7000

- Be prepared to provide your FAN (Foundation Account Number)

- Initial call information will be referred to the FirstNet Response Operations Group at AT&T who will process the request on behalf of AT&T

FirstNet Central: Uplift Portal and Incident Management
firstnetcentral.firstnet.com

FirstNet Central is a web portal for FirstNet's public safety users and offers a collection of administrative tools, training resources, and operational tools on a single platform. FirstNet Central is designed to help public safety and emergency management entities with increased situational awareness, identify potential impact to operations, and guide decisions on use of resources.

The Network Status Map, including an Advanced Network View, provides FirstNet public safety users the ability to view the status of the network, and offers additional information and features that can be customized by the user, including the ability to view cell site level detail. Users can subscribe to receive alerts for unplanned network outages via text, e-mail, or push notification to the FirstNet Assist app.

The Uplift Request Tool can be used by designated Uplift Managers to temporarily raise the tier of a FirstNet device (any device provisioned with a FirstNet SIM) to grant all three benefits of Quality of Service, Priority, and Preemption (QPP). FirstNet Primary users (EMS, Fire, Law Enforcement, Emergency Communications, Emergency Management) always have the highest level of QPP or "First Priority®." Through the Uplift Request Tool, FirstNet Extended Primary users (e.g., public works, utilities, debris removal, etc.) can be temporarily elevated when supporting first responders is critical, granting them the same levels of QPP experienced by Primary users. Uplift requests can be created and launched immediately, or they can be scheduled up to one year in advance for a planned event.

FirstNet Assist App
firstnet.com/apps/featured-apps/firstnet-assist.html

FirstNet Assist is a free mobile app for Apple iOS or Android that is used to access or interact with different elements of FirstNet Central. The FirstNet Assist app is accessed using the same login as FirstNet Central. Users can check the app to see if there are any Uplift Incidents tied to the incident or event they are responding to, and request to have their device uplifted if desired.

T-Mobile Emergency Response Team

Dedicated Support Line: 888-639-0020
GETS Users: 254-295-2220
Email: ERTRequests@T-Mobile.com

T-Mobile is prepared and ready to provide data, voice and cellular solutions to organizations within incident impacted areas and groups responding to the areas devastated by any incident. T-Mobile stands ready to assist during response and recovery efforts.

Services Offered:

- Mobile infrastructure for cellular service – Cells on Wheels (COWs), Cells on Light Trucks (COLTs), Satellite-connected Cells on Light Trucks (SatCOLTs), and Small Cell solutions
- Satellite-connected deployables - VSAT (Satellite Antenna), Satellite IP Trailers
- Mobile Command Trailers
- Satellite performance up to 45 Mbps downlink x 10 Mbps Wireline Connection (Ethernet)
- Wireline Connection (Ethernet)
- Commercial WiFi
- Basic Phones, Smartphones, and Hotspots
- CradlePoint Routers
- Mutualink Interoperability solution

Verizon Response Team

Nationwide 24/7/365 Support Line: 800-981-9885

verizon.com/business/solutions/public-sector/public-safety/programs/verizon-response-team/

Verizon Response Team is a national, rapid deploy, professionally trained team who solve routine and complex communication challenges in all environments.

Services Offered:

- Mobile communications equipment – Cells on Wheels (COWs), Cells on Light Trucks (COLTs), and Satellite Picocell on Trailers

- Satellite-connected deployables - VSAT (Satellite Antenna), Satellite IP Trailers

- Rugged deployables – Purpose-built, weatherproof, military grade with a built in 4G LTE solution that combines high-power charging mAh battery.

- Drones – UAS 107 Licensed Drone Program across the U.S. that provides situational awareness during an event.

- Loaner phones and data devices

- Enterprise-grade 4G LTE routers with directional antenna solutions

- Emergency communication and charging centers

- Pre-event planning and site assessments

- Verizon Security Assistance Team support – missing persons/search and rescue

Telephone Keypad Letters		
1: (QZ)	2: ABC	3: DEF
4: GHI	5: JKL	6: MNO
7: P(Q)RS	8: TUV	9: WXY(Z)
*	0	#

N11 Numbers	
N11 Code	Description
2-1-1	Community information and referral services
3-1-1	Non-emergency police and other government services
4-1-1	Directory assistance
5-1-1	Traffic and transportation information
6-1-1	Repair service
7-1-1	Telecommunications relay services
8-1-1	Utility excavation notification - "Call Before You Dig"
9-1-1	Emergency services

nationalnanpa.com/number_resource_info/n11_codes.html

DSN Area Codes

Defense Switched Network - Global Operator – 1-719-567-1110
(DSN 312-560-1110)

disa.mil/Network-Services/Voice/SBU-Voice/Using-DSN/DSN-Tutorial/Area-Codes

312 – CONUS	313 – Caribbean
314 – Europe	315 – Pacific
317 – Alaska	318 – Southwest Asia
319 – Canada	

DSN Directory - Global

disa.mil/network-services/voice/sbu-voice/directory

Text Messaging

"number" is the 10-digit mobile telephone number, unless 11-digit-number is specified

Selected US & Canadian Cellular Text Messaging Carriers

Alltel	**SMS:** number@sms.alltelwireless.com **MMS:** number@mms.alltelwireless.com
AT&T	**SMS:** number@txt.att.net **MMS:** number@mms.att.net
Bell Canada	**SMS & MMS:** number@txt.bell.ca
Boost Mobile	**SMS:** number@sms.myboostmobile.com **MMS:** number@myboostmobile.com
C Spire Wireless	**SMS & MMS:** number@cspire.com
Cricket Wireless	**SMS:** number@sms.mycricket.com **SMS:** number@sms.cricketwireless.net **MMS:** number@mms.mycricket.com **MMS:** number@mms.cricketwireless.net
FirstNet	**SMS:** number@sms.firstnet-mail.com **MMS:** number@txt.firstnet-mail.com
Metro PCS	**SMS & MMS:** number@mymetropcs.com or number@metropcs.sms.us
Qwest	**SMS & MMS:** number@qwestmp.com
SouthernLinc Wireless	**SMS:** number@page.southernlinc.com **MMS:** number@mms.southernlinc.com
Sprint	**SMS & MMS:** number@messaging.sprintpcs.com or number@pm.sprint.com
T-Mobile	**SMS & MMS:** 10-digit-number@tmomail.net

(continued on next page)

Text Messaging

Telus Mobility	**SMS & MMS:** number@msg.telus.com **MMS:** number@mms.telusmobility.com
TracFone	**SMS & MMS:** number@mmst5.tracfone.com
U.S. Cellular	**SMS:** number@email.uscc.net **MMS:** number@mms.uscc.net
Verizon	**SMS:** number@vtext.com **MMS:** number@vzwpix.com
Virgin Mobile	**SMS:** number@vmobl.com **MMS:** number@vmpix.com
Alaska	
Alaska Communications	**SMS:** number@txt.acsalaska.net **MMS:** 11-digit-number@mms.ak.net
General Communications Inc. (GCI)	**SMS:** number@mobile.gci.net **MMS:** number@mms.gci.net
Puerto Rico	
Centennial Wireless	**SMS:** number@cwemail.com
Claro	**SMS:** number@vtexto.com
TracFone	**SMS:** number@mmst5.tracfone.com
U.S. Virgin Islands	
Centennial Wireless	**SMS:** number@cwemail.com
TracFone	**MMS:** number@mmst5.tracfone.com
Worldwide	
Iridium	**SMS:** number@msg.iridium.com

SATELLITE SERVICES

M-SAT Satellite Mutual Aid Radio Talkgroups (SMART™)

The Satellite Mutual Aid Radio Talkgroup program, is a satellite- based Push-to-Talk (PTT) service operating over the Ligado MSAT Network connecting federal, state, local and tribal public safety users of the MSAT Network via seven national discipline-specific Talkgroups and nine regional Talkgroups. The primary use of these Talkgroups is for interoperable communications among agencies during both pre-planned and emergency events.

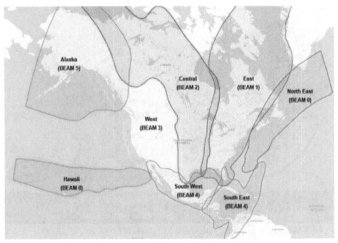

Figure 6 - Ligado Networks SMART Talkgroups Coverage Map

Operational Support Information

Ligado Networks 24/7 Operations Center	Network Innovations 24/7 Technical Support
Toll Free: 1-800-216-6728 Toll: 1-703-390-2755 support@ligado.com	Toll Free: 1-888-664-6727 Toll: 1-954-973-3100 - Opt. 3) support@networkinv.com

ligado.com/solutions/msat-satellite-services/smart-program/

Nationwide SMART Talkgroups	
Talkgroup	Discipline
J-SMART	Public Safety
L-SMART	Law Enforcement
F-SMART	Fire Service
E-SMART	EMS
U-SMART	Urban Search & Rescue
I-SMART	Critical Infrastructure
NPHST-2	Public Health

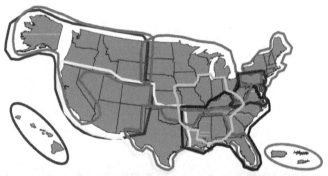

Regional SMART Talkgroups	
Talkgroup	States/Territories
NESMART	CT, DE, MA, ME, NH, NY, NJ, PA, RI, and VT
M-SMART	DC, DE, MD, PA, VA, and WV
SESMART	AL, AR, FL, GA, KY, LA, MS, NC, SC, TN, VA, and WV
G-SMART	AL, FL, LA, MS, TX, PR, and VI
MWSMART	IA, IL, IN, KS, KY, MI, MN, MO, OH, ND, NE, SD, WI, and WV
SWSMART	AZ, CA, CO, NV, NM, OK, TX, and UT
W-SMART	AK, AZ, CA, CO, HI, ID, MT, NM, NV, OR, UT, WA, and WY
NWSMART	AK, CA, ID, MT, OR, WA, and WY
CUSEC-1	AL, AR, IL, IN, KY, MS, MO, and TN

Satellite Phone Dialing Instructions

IRIDIUM

Iridium PIN (default) is 1111

(enter when powering-on the Iridium Subscriber Unit)

From a US Landline

Two-Stage Dialing: 1-480-768-2500, at prompt 12-digit Iridium number

To an Iridium phone directly as an International Call
011 + 8816xxxxxxx (Iridium Phone Number)

To an Iridium phone via toll call to Chandler AZ ("two-stage dialing"):
1-480-768-2500, follow prompts to enter Iridium phone number

From a Iridium provisioned commercially

To a US Phone number
00 + 1 + xxx.xxx.xxxx (US phone number)

To an Iridium phone directly
00 + 8816xxxxxxx (Iridium Phone Number)

Test call - no airtime charge: 00 + 1 + 480.752.5105

From a Iridium provisioned by DOD

ISU (Iridium Subscriber Unit) to DSN

00 + 696 + (DSN Area Code) + (DSN 7-digit number)

ISU to U.S. Domestic

00 + 697 + (U.S. Area Code) + (7-digit US number)

ISU to International Long Distance (ILD)

00 + 698 + (Country Code) + ("National Destination Code" or
"City Code") + (Subscriber Number)

ISU to INMARSAT

00 + 698 + 870 + (INMARSAT subscriber number)

ISU to Local Hawaii

00 + 699 + (7-digit local commercial number)
1-800 toll-free   00 + 699 + 1+ 800 + (7-digits)

ISU to ISU, handset-to-handset

00 + (12-digit ISU subscriber number, e.g., 8816 763-xxxxx)

BGAN

From a BGAN: [Note - Cannot call Toll-Free numbers]

To a US Phone number:

00 + 1 + (10-digit US phone number) + #

To an Iridium phone directly

00 + 8816xxxxxxx (Iridium Phone Number) + #

MSAT

From a Ligado MSAT:

To a US Phone number:

(10-digit US phone number) + SEND

To an International number

011 + (Country Code) + (Exchange) + (Number) + SEND

Using GETS Dialing

1-272-627-4387 + SEND, Pin number at tone, follow prompt then enter (10-digit US Number or International Number)

INMARSAT

INMARSAT Country Code

All INMARSAT satellite telephones now use country code 870.

The Ocean Region Codes were discontinued January 1, 2009:

871   Atlantic Ocean Region – East [AOR-East]
872   Pacific Ocean Region [POR]
873   Indian Ocean Region [IOR]
874   Atlantic Ocean Region – West [AOR-West]

Inmarsat Customer Care Helpline - international direct dialing from USA to London, United Kingdom: 011 44 20 7728 1030

INMARSAT-M Service Codes

00	Automatic Calls
11	International Operator
12	International Information
13	National Operator
14	National Information
17	Telephone Call Booking
20	Access to a Maritime PAD
23	Abbreviated Dialing
24	Post FAX
31	Maritime Enquiries
32	Medical Advice
33	Technical Assistance
34	Person-to-Person Call
35	Collect Call
36	Credit Card Call
37	Time and Duration
38	Medical Assistance
39	Maritime Assistance
41	Meteorological Reports
42	Navigational Hazards and Warnings
43	Ship Position Reports
57	Retrieval of Mailbox Messages
6x	Administration, Specialized Use
70	Databases
91	Automatic Line Test
911	Emergency Calls
92	Commissioning Tests

INFORMATION TECHNOLOGY

Network Troubleshooting*

Network	Fault Domain	Potential Causes
Wireless LAN	End User	Perception, lack of knowledge
	User Device	Drivers, Overloaded CPU/RAM, Resource contention, corporate security policies, installed tools
	RF Medium	RSSI/SNR, Spectral Interference, Incorrect/Missing Antenna, DFS conflict resolution
	Association	Incorrect configuration, de-authentication/dis-associate, incorrect roaming, incompatible hardware
	Authentication	Incorrect configuration, incompatible hardware, no connection to RADIUS
	Access Point	SSID, minimum basic rate, band steering, client isolation, roaming, incorrect mounting, PoE, VLAN trunk
Wired LAN	Physical Layer	Electrical interference, incorrect termination, 568A/B mismatch, grounding, line break
	Switching	VLANs, QoS, Duplex mismatch, spanning tree, resource contention
	Transport	TCP window size, round trip time, packet loss, retransmission times, MTU size, congestion, IP conflict
	VLANs	Native vs tagged port, VLAN assignments, DHCP, QoS mismatch
	DHCP	Lease duration, pool size, broadcast storms, rogue DHCP server
	DNS	Resource contention, forwarding and recursion, missing entry
	Firewall	Rule-base, cache size, traffic shaping, Deep Packet Inspection, IDS/IPS, asynchronous route
	Routing	Subnet conflict, route cost, firewall rule, routing table size
Internet	Connection	Bandwidth throttling, link latency, packet loss, priority and preemption service outage
	Availability	Weather, service outage, account status

This table should be used from top to bottom

Information Technology Disaster Resource Center

The Information Technology Disaster Resource Center (ITDRC) is a nationwide, volunteer driven 501(c)3 organization that leverages volunteers from across the technology sector to deploy solutions immediately following a natural disaster. Founded in 2008, ITDRC provides immediate technical assistance to communities impacted by disasters free of charge.

Each year, ITDRC volunteers contribute tens of thousands of hours providing temporary resources and technical assistance to communities impacted by fires, floods, tornadoes, and hurricanes; and we continue to support them through long term recovery. The team maintains 5 equipment caches across the US and Puerto Rico. ITDRC has satisfied over 3000 technology-based solution requests helping over 1200 communities nationwide.

ITDRC is a National VOAD member, a charter FEMA Tech Sector Collaboration Partner, and trusted resource to Emergency Management agencies and national NGOs across the country.

For more information, please visit itdrc.org or email support@itdrc.org

24/7 Activation Hotline: 866.217.5777

Services Offered:

- Internet/Wifi Support
- IMT Deployment Support to Communications Unit(s)
- Mobile Command Centers
- Temporary EOC infrastructure
- Laptop cache
- Cyber Incident Response Support
- Internet cafes for responder rehab, shelter residents
- Phones for Incident Command, Volunteer Reception Center, or Long-Term Recovery Center

Cisco Crisis Response (formerly Tactical Operations)

Cisco Crisis Response provides temporary, mission-critical voice, data and video service to first responder, state, local, and Federal agencies, critical infrastructure and humanitarian aid organizations. Services may be provided for pre-planned and disaster incidents, subject to availability. This is a best-effort, pro-bono service.

For additional information see cisco.com/go/tacops or email tacops-info@cisco.com

Emergency Contact Information

Email: emergencyresponse@cisco.com 24x7 Hotline: 1-919-392-4646

Be prepared to provide:

- Requesting individual's name, agency, title, phone, email
- Exact location(s) of incident
- Business need (e.g., telephone, internet, radio interoperability)
- Approximate number of users
- Expected duration
- Current ground situation re: logistics, security, personnel support etc.

Open Source Interconnection (OSI) Seven Layer Model

Layer Name	Encapsulation	Purpose	Common Devices	Standards/Protocols
Application		Interface to the user	User Applications	HTTP, SMTP, DHCP, BGP, TFTP, SSH
Presentation	Data	Character code translation, compression, encryption	JPG, ASCII	Radius, Kerberos, TACACS
Session		Session Establishment, Management, and Termination	RPC, NFS, NetBIOS Naming	PPTP, L2TP, L2F
Transport	Segments or Datagrams	Stateful and Stateless Delivery, Flow Control		TCP, UDP, NetBIOS
Network	Packets	Logical Addressing, Routing	Router, Firewall, Layer 3 Switch	IPv4, IPv6, IPX, ICMP, IGMP
Data Link	Frames	Physical Addressing, Sequencing, Error Checking, Media Access Control	Switch, Bridge, Wireless AP	802.11a/b/g/n, Frame Relay, IEEE802.3 CSMA/CD, MPLS, ARP, ATM
Physical	Bits	Data encoding across the physical medium	OM2 Fiber, CAT6 Copper, 2.4 GHZ	IEEE802.3, IEEE802.11, SONET, PAM, BPSK, QPSK, 64QAM

Physical Media for Data Networks

Category	Media	Shielding	Max Distance	Max Speed	Connector	Interference	Cost	Typical Use
Coax	RG-8	Dual	500 m	10 Mbps	F-Type	Low	Medium	Legacy Network
	RG-58	Single	185 m	10 Mbps	F-Type	Low	Medium	Legacy Network
	CAT3	No	100 m	10 Mbps	RJ-11	High	Very Low	Telephone
Twisted Copper Pair	CAT5	No	100 m	100 Mbps	RJ-45	Medium	Low	Legacy Network
	CAT5e	No	100 m	1 Gbps	RJ-45	Medium	Low	Voice and Data Network
	CAT6	Optional	100 m	1 Gbps	RJ-45	Low-Medium	Medium	Voice and Data Network
	CAT6a	Yes	100 m	10 Gbps	RJ-45	Low-Medium	Medium	Data Center / Campus Wiring
	CAT7	Yes	100 m	10 Gbps	RJ-45	Low	Medium	Data Center / Campus Wiring
	CAT8	Yes	100 m	40 Gbps	RJ-45	Low	Medium	Data Center / Campus Wiring
Multi-Mode Fiber Optic	OM1	Yes	550 m	10 Gbps	SC, LC, ST	Low	Medium	Data Center Networks
	OM2	Yes	550 m	10 Gbps	SC, LC, ST	Low	Medium	Data Center / Storage Networks
	OM3	Yes	800 m	100 Gbps	SC, LC, ST	Low	Medium	Campus / Metropolitan WAN
	OM4	Yes	800 m	100 Gbps	SC, LC, ST	Low	High	Campus / Metropolitan WAN
	OM5	Yes	400 m	100 Gbps	SC, LC, ST	Low	High	Campus / Metropolitan WAN
Single Mode Fiber Optic	OS1	Yes	10 km	10 Gbps	SC, LC, ST	Very Low	Very High	ISP / Telephone Infrastructure
	OS2	Yes	40 km	100 Gbps	SC, LC, ST	Very Low	Very High	ISP / Telephone Infrastructure
RF	2.4 GHz	N/A	90m	54 Mbps	N/A	High	NA	Wireless Data Networking
	5 GHz	N/A	30m	866 Mbps	N/A	High	NA	Wireless Data Networking

Public DNS Servers IPv4 & IPv6

Domain Name System (DNS) is a decentralized service that translates human understandable hostnames and Universal Resource Locators (URL) into IP addresses usable by lower level network protocols.

DNS is facilitated through the use of four different types of server roles. These servers operate in a hierarchical structure to coordinate query responses. The four roles include:

Recursive Resolvers – this role is used to receive resolution requests from clients. It attempts to respond from its cache of previous responses before searching for an authoritative response

Root Name Servers – there are 13 root name servers to direct requests from recursive resolvers to the appropriate TLD server (e.g. .com, .net, etc.) for the domain being requested

TLD Name Server – these servers direct the recursive resolver to an authoritative name server for the domain being requested

Authoritative Name Server – this server is designated by the owner of a domain to host the original zone files for all records associated with the specified domain and provide definitive answers to all queries

Several different types of DNS records are used to correctly identify the IP address associated with the service being requested. The most common DNS record types include:

A	This record holds the IPv4 address of a domain or host
AAAA	This record resolves the IPv6 address (similar to A records)
CNAME	The entry is an alias for a different record
MX	Directs mail to the domain email servers
SRV	Identifies both the IP address and network port for a service
PTR	Enables "reverse look-ups" for names associated with IPs

The TLD name servers are managed by the Internet Corporation for Assigned Names and Numbers (ICANN). They are located around the world. All recursive resolver servers should use the following servers:

Hostname	IPv4 Address	IPv6 Address
a.root-servers.net	198.41.0.4	2001:503:ba3e::2:30
b.root-servers.net	199.9.14.201	2001:500:200::b
c.root-servers.net	192.33.4.12	2001:500:2::c
d.root-servers.net	199.7.91.13	2001:500:2d::d
e.root-servers.net	192.203.230.10	2001:500:a8::e
f.root-servers.net	192.5.5.241	2001:500:2f::f
g.root-servers.net	192.112.36.4	2001:500:12::d0d
h.root-servers.net	198.97.190.53	2001:500:1::53
i.root-servers.net	192.36.148.17	2001:7fe::53
j.root-servers.net	192.58.128.30	2001:503:c27::2:30
k.root-servers.net	193.0.14.129	193.0.14.129
l.root-servers.net	199.7.83.42	2001:500:9f::42
m.root-servers.net	202.12.27.33	2001:dc3::35

Many reputable providers offer DNS services to the public. The following list provides several commonly used providers. It should not be construed as an endorsement.

Provider	IP Version	Primary	Secondary
Cloudflare	IPv4	1.1.1.1	1.0.0.1
	IPv6	2606:4700:4700::1111	2606:4700:4700::1001
Comodo	IPv4	8.26.56.26	8.20.247.20
FreeDNS	IPv4	37.235.1.174	37.235.1.177
Google	IPv4	8.8.8.8	8.8.4.4
	IPv6	2001:4860:4860::8888	2001:4860:4860::8844
Level 3	IPv4	4.2.2.1	4.2.2.2
OpenDNS (Umbrella)	IPv4	208.67.222.222	208.67.220.220
	IPv6	2620:0:ccc::2	2620:0:ccd::2
OpenNIC	IPv4	185.121.177.177	169.239.202.202
	IPv6	2a05:dfc7:5::53	2a05:dfc7:5353::53
Quad9	IPv4	9.9.9.9	149.112.112.112
	IPv6	2620:fe::fe	2620:fe::9

Reserved Address Spaces

RFC1122 – This Host: 0.0.0.0/8

This address space is reserved self-identification when request an IP address using the Dynamic Host Control Protocol (DHCP) and to indicate "all IP addresses on this host" in kernel routing and service listeners.

    Loopback: 127.0.0.1

This address space is reserved to direct a datagram created by any higher-level protocol with a destination address in this block to the local machine itself.

RFC1918 – Private Use: 10.0.0.0/8

        172.16.0.0/12

        192.168.0.0/16

These blocks are reserved for routable assignments on any private networks with no intention of directly connecting to other networks over the Internet.

RFC3927 – Link-Local: 169.254.0.0/16

The addresses in this block are available to allow a host to automatically assign itself an IP address for use in connecting with other devices on the same logical network when it fails to obtain an IP address from a source using the Dynamic Host Control Protocol (DHCP)

RFC3171 – Multicast: 224.0.0.0/4

This block of addresses is reserved to facilitate the delivery of one-to-many and many-to-many transmissions across the network.

Subnetting / CIDR Notation

Classful networks were introduced in 1981 as a part of RFC-791 defining the specification for the Internet Protocol. The address space was divided into 3 address formats with a 4th to be defined later known as address classes. This approach did not provide efficient use of the address space. RFC-971 was introduced in 1984 to provide the concept of a subnet mask to subdivide classes into a network identifier and a host identifier. Address classes are only useful to know from a historical perspective. They were obsoleted in 1993 with the introduction of RFC-1518 (later updated in 2006 by RFC-4632) for Classless Inter-Domain Routing (CIDR).

CIDR provides a method for representing IP address space using a bitwise, prefix-based standard to define which portion of an IPv4 address identifies a network and which identifies individual hosts. For example, a subnet mask of 255.255.252.0 indicates the first 22 bits of the IP address will identify the network and the remainder will identify hosts. CIDR notation is a short-hand representation of the network address and the subnet mask e.g., aaa.bbb.ccc.0/24.

CIDR Block	Mask	Usable Addresses	Typical Use
/32	255.255.255.255	1	Host Only
/31	255.255.255.254	2	RFC3021
/30	255.255.255.252	2	Point-to-Point
/29	255.255.255.248	6	Smallest multi-host LAN
/28	255.255.255.240	14	Small LAN
/27	255.255.255.224	30	
/26	255.255.255.192	62	
/25	255.255.255.128	126	Large LAN
/24	255.255.255.0	254	
/23	255.255.254.0	510	Small Business
/22	255.255.252.0	1022	Medium Business
/21	255.255.248.0	2046	Small ISP
/20	255.255.240.0	4094	Large Business
/19	255.255.224.0	8190	
/18	255.255.192.0	16382	Medium ISP
/17	255.255.128.0	65534	
/16	255.255.0.0	131070	Large ISP

Public Network Time Protocol (NTP) Servers

Others are available, no endorsement implied.

Domain Name	IP Address
0.pool.ntp.org	(randomly assigned)
1.pool.ntp.org	(randomly assigned)
2.pool.ntp.org	(randomly assigned)
3.pool.ntp.org	(randomly assigned)
tick.usno.navy.mil	192.5.41.40
tock.usno.navy.mil	192.5.41.41
bigben.cac.washington.edu	140.142.16.34
ntp-nasa.arc.nasa.gov	198.123.30.132

Examples of Troubleshooting with Packet Captures

Task	Wireshark Filter[*]	TCPDump[**]
Filter for a specific host	ip.addr == [IP address]	tcpdump host [IP address]
Filter for a specific subnet	ip.addr == [Network in CIDR notation]	tcpdump net [Network in CIDR notation]
Filter for a specific TCP port	tcp.port == [port number]	tcpdump tcp port [port number]
Filter for a specific UDP port	udp.port == [port number]	tcpdump udp port [port number]
Filter packets less than length	frame.len < [byte length]	tcpdump less [byte length]
Filter packets greater than length	frame.len > [byte length]	tcpdump greater [byte length]
Filter for specific URL	http.host == [URL]	tcpdump tcp port 80 and host [URL]
Find specific text in the datagram	frame contains [text to match]	tcpdump -vvls0	grep -i [text to match]
Filter on Wifi SSID	wlan_mgt.ssid == [SSID]	tcpdump -vvel subtype beacon	grep [SSID]
Logical Operators		
Equal	command == [expression]	And	command && [expression]
Not Equal	command != [expression]	Or	command || [expression]
Greater Than	command > [expression]	Less Than	command < [expression]
Greater Than Equal To	command >= [expression]	Less Than Equal To	command <= [expression]

Important Note: The collection of network traffic may violate local and federal laws and/or corporate and departmental regulations and policies. Permission should be obtained from an authorized representative for a network owner prior to performing any collections.

[*] may require elevated or administrator privileges   [**] may require root or pseudo access

Comparison of Common VPN Protocols

	Point-to-Point Tunneling Protocol (PPTP)	Internet Key Exchange v2 (IKEV2)	Layer 2 Tunneling Protocol (L2TP)	Secure Socket Tunneling Protocol (SSTP)	OpenVPN
Encryption	RC4 (40/128 bit)	3DES and AES-256	AES-256	AES-256	AES-256
Transport	PPP over GRE	IPSec	IPSec	HTTPS	Proprietary
TCP/UDP Port	TCP 1723	IP 50/51 and UDP 500/4500	UDP 1701	TCP 443	TCP 443 or UDP 1194
Security	Has several well-known vulnerabilities	Implements IPSec and is very secure	Implements IPSec; weakened by poor configuration	Implements TLS and is very secure	Considered the most secure, no known vulnerabilities
Stability	TCP-based VPNs are prone to frequent disconnection	Highly stable once a connection is established	Very stable	Very stable, especially on Windows	Very stable when using UDP
Speed	Fast	Fast	Fast	Medium	Slow
Compatibility	Client built into most operating systems	Generally available on most platforms	Generally available on most platforms	Windows and Mac OS	Client and server software available for most platforms
Proxy Support	No	No	No	Yes	Yes
Firewall Bypass	Requires open ports	Requires open ports	Requires open ports	Easily bypassed	Easily bypassed
Common Uses	Easy of deployment	Site-to-Site Connections	More secure remote client access	Easy of bypassing firewalls	Strong security

WAN Technologies / Common Data Rates

WAN Technology	Typical Bandwidth	Latency (ms)	Cost	Reliability	Security	Suitability			
						Video	Voice	GIS	Web
Corporate	100+ Mbps	10-20	Low	Medium	Very Low	Good	Good	Good	Good
Public Wifi	40-50 Mbps	25-30	Low	Medium	Very Low	Good	Good	Good	Good
DSL	50-100 Mbps	20-30	Medium	High	High	Good	Good	Good	Good
Cable Modem	200+ Mbps	15-20	Medium	High	High	Good	Good	Good	Good
Cellular	40-50 Mbps	30-40	Med-High	Medium	High	Ok	Good	Good	Good
VSat	7/2 Mbps	500-700	Medium	Medium	Med-High	Poor	Ok	Poor	Good
BGAN	756 Kbps	80-100	Very High	Medium	Med-High	Poor	Poor	Poor	Good
LoRaWAN	200 Kbps	300-400	Low	Medium	Medium	Poor	Poor	Poor	Ok

Understanding WAN Performance

Bandwidth –the capacity of a link measured by the volume of data that be transferred per unit of time

Latency – the speed of a link measured by the time it takes for data to travel from point A to point B

Packet Loss – the percentage of data that failed to successfully arrive at the destination

Throughput – the actual volume of data transferred per unit of time after latency and packet loss

Jitter – the average duration in milliseconds caused by packet arriving at the destination out of sequence

Path Asymmetry – the net throughput caused by variations in performance between the up and down link

WAN Considerations

How many people will use the network? Plan for 1.5 Mbps per user

What applications will be used over the network? Certain applications are more sensitive to WAN performance

What are the security considerations? VPN protocols can be sensitive to WAN performance.

North America WIFI Channel Plan and Best Practices

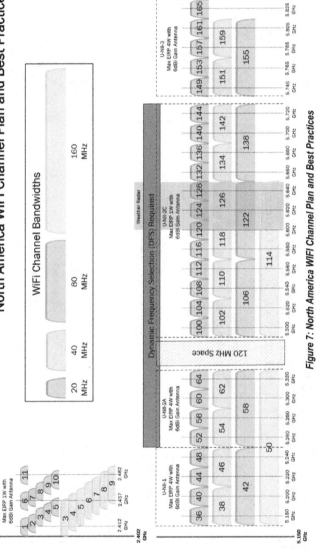

Figure 7: North America WIFI Channel Plan and Best Practices

WIFI Configuration Best Practices

	2.4 GHz	5.8 GHz
Protocol	802.11 g/n only	802.11 a/n/ac
SSID Hidden	No	
Client Isolation	Enabled for guest networks	
WMM	Disabled unless media streaming is important	
Security Mode	WPA2 / WPA3	
Encryption Method	AES Only	
Channel Selection	Fixed Install: See Figures 1 & 2 Mobile: Auto Channel Selection	
RTS Threshold	534 bytes	
Fragmentation Threshold	784 bytes	
DTIM	1	
Beacon	100ms	
Management Frame Protection	Enabled	
Airtime Fairness	Disabled	
Channel Width	20 MHz	40 MHz
Fast Roaming	Enabled	

Figure 8: 2.4 GHz Channel Adjacency for High Density Deployments

Figure 9: 5 GHz Channel Adjacency for High Density Deployments

RJ-45 Pinout

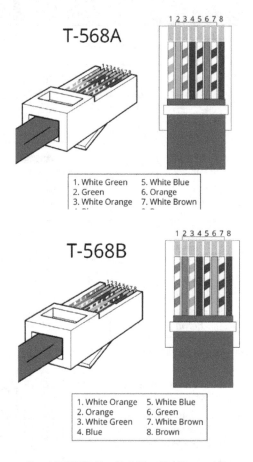

T-568A

1. White Green	5. White Blue
2. Green	6. Orange
3. White Orange	7. White Brown

T-568B

1. White Orange	5. White Blue
2. Orange	6. Green
3. White Green	7. White Brown
4. Blue	8. Brown

Figure 10: RJ-45 Pinout

RJ-45 Wiring

Pin	T568A Pair	T568A Color	T568A Signal	T568 B Pair	T568B Color	T568B Signal
1	3	White / Green	RX Data + (RD+)	2	White / Orange	TX Data + (TD+)
2	3	Green	RX Data – (RX–)	2	Orange	TX Data – (TD–)
3	2	White / Orange	TX Data + (TD+)	3	White / Green	RX Data + (RD+)
4	1	Blue		1	Blue	
5	1	White / Blue		1	White / Blue	
6	2	Orange	TX Data – (TD–)	3	Green	RX Data – (RX–)
7	4	White / Brown		4	White / Brown	
8	4	Brown		4	Brown	

- T568B is more commonly used than T568A
- Odd pin numbers are always with the "white-with-strip" color
- A straight cable has both ends the same:
  • Both T568A (Older Standard)
  • Both T568B (Newer Standard)
- A crossover cable has one end wired as T568A and the other as T568B

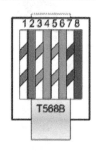

1 2 3 4 5 6 7 8

T568B

Telephone Connectors

Pin numbers are from left to right, holding the plug with the contacts up and looking at the side that does not have the spring clip. "T" and "R" indicate "Tip" and "Ring."

Pin	RJ11 6P2C	RJ14 6P4C	RJ25 6P6C	U.S. Bell System Colors	25-pair Color Code
1			T3	White	White/Green
2		T2	T2	Black	White/Orange
3	R1	R1	R1	Red	Blue/White
4	T1	T1	T1	Green	White/Blue
5		R2	R2	Yellow	Orange/White
6			R3	Blue	Green/White

RJ-11, RJ-14, and RJ-25 Connector Wiring

Looking into female 6P6C connector with pins on the top.

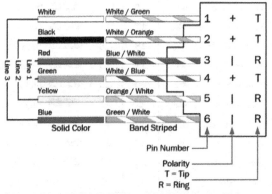

Figure 11: RJ-11, RJ-14, and RJ-25 Connector Wiring

25 Pair Telephone Block Wiring Color Code

Color	Tip	Pair	Ring	Color
White/Blue	26	**1**	1	Blue/White
White/Orange	27	**2**	2	Orange/White
White/Green	28	**3**	3	Green/White
White/Brown	29	**4**	4	Brown/White
White/Slate	30	**5**	5	Slate/White
Red/Blue	31	**6**	6	Blue/Red
Red/Orange	32	**7**	7	Orange/Red
Red/Green	33	**8**	8	Green/Red
Red/Brown	34	**9**	9	Brown/Red
Red/Slate	35	**10**	10	Slate/Red
Black/Blue	36	**11**	11	Blue/Black
Black/Orange	37	**12**	12	Orange/Black
Black/Green	38	**13**	13	Green/Black
Black/Brown	39	**14**	14	Brown/Black
Black/Slate	40	**15**	15	Slate/Black
Yellow/Blue	41	**16**	16	Blue/Yellow
Yellow/Orange	42	**17**	17	Orange/Yellow
Yellow/Green	43	**18**	18	Green/Yellow
Yellow/Brown	44	**19**	19	Brown/Yellow
Yellow/Slate	45	**20**	20	Slate/Yellow
Violet/Blue	46	**21**	21	Blue/Violet
Violet/Orange	47	**22**	22	Orange/Violet
Violet/Green	48	**23**	23	Green/Violet
Violet/Brown	49	**24**	24	Brown/Violet
Violet/Slate	50	**25**	25	Slate/Violet

Notes on Fiber Optic Cable and Connectors

ANSI/TIA/EIA-598-B Standard Colors	
Fiber #	Color
1	Blue
2	Orange
3	Green
4	Brown
5	Slate
6	White
7	Rose
8	Black
9	Yellow
10	Violet
11	Rose
12	Aqua

13 and higher:
The color code is repeated,
Black stripe or dash is added,
according to the ANSI/TIA/EIA-598-B specs.

LC

SC

ST

- All fiber optic cable is not the same. There are two major types in typical field use: Single-Mode and Multi-Mode

- Single-Mode is common for long haul fiber runs

- Multi-Mode is more common to short runs, i.e., LAN

- There are numerous connectors in use; the most common are LC, SC and ST

- Know the fiber type requirement of the terminal equipment

- Know the connectors of terminal equipment

- Plan for the physical protection of a tactical fiber deployment

RS-232 Connectors (DE9 and DB25)

"Front" refers to the ends with the pins; "rear" refers to the end with the cable. The following is a view of the pins, looking at the front of the female connector (rear of male):

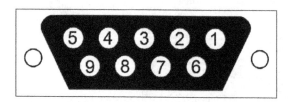

same for DB25, except top pins 13 - 1, bottom 25 - 14 (right to left)

DE9	DB25	Signal
1	8	Carrier Detect
2	3	Receive Data
3	2	Transmit Data*
4	20	Data Terminal Ready*
5	1,7	Ground **
6	6	Data Set Ready
7	4	Request to Send*
8	5	Clear to Send
9	22	Ring Indicator

* An output from the computer to the outside world.

** On the DB25, 1 is the protective ground, 7 is the signal ground.

Uniform Color Code of Underground Utility Markings

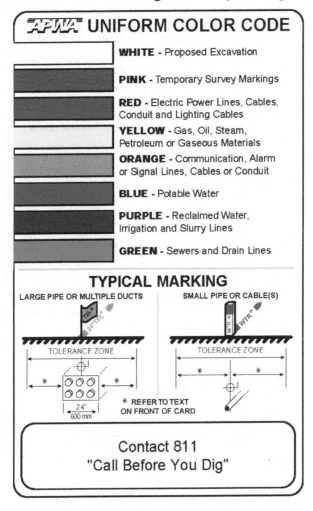

GUIDELINES FOR UNIFORM TEMPORARY MARKING OF UNDERGROUND FACILITIES

This marking guide provides for universal use and understanding of the temporary marking of subsurface facilities to prevent accidents and damage or service interruption by contractors, excavators, utility companies, municipalities or any others working on or near underground facilities.

ONE-CALL SYSTEMS
The One-Call damage prevention system shall be contacted prior to excavation.

PROPOSED EXCAVATION
Use white marks to show the location, route or boundary of proposed excavation. Surface marks on roadways do not exceed 1.5" by 18" (40 mm by 450 mm). The facility color and facility owner identity may be added to white flags or stakes.

USE OF TEMPORARY MARKING
Use color-coded surface marks (i.e., paint or chalk) to indicate the location or route of active and out-of-service buried lines. To increase visibility, color coded vertical markers (i.e., stakes or flags) should supplement surface marks. Marks and markers indicate the name, initials or logo of the company that owns or operates the line, and width of the facility if it is greater than 2" (50 mm). Marks placed by other than line owner/operator or its agent indicate the identity of the designating firm. Multiple lines in joint trench are marked in tandem. If the surface over the buried line is to be removed, supplementary offset markings are used. Offset markings are on a uniform alignment and clearly indicate the actual facility is a specific distance away.

TOLERANCE ZONE
Any excavation within the tolerance zone is performed with non-powered hand tools or non-invasive method until the marked facility is exposed. The width of the tolerance zone may be specified in law or code. If not, a tolerance zone including the width of the facility plus 18" (450 mm) measured horizontally from each side of the facility is recommended.

ADOPT UNIFORM COLOR CODE
The American Public Works Association encourages public agencies, utilities, contractors, other associations, manufacturers and all others involved in excavation to adopt the APWA Uniform Color Code, using ANSI standard Z535.1 Safety Colors for temporary marking and facility identification.

Rev. 4/99

Figure 12: Uniform Color Code of Underground Utility Markings

CYBERSECURITY

Top Cybersecurity Tactics

User Education

- Have the users been briefed on cyber hygiene?
- Are the users aware how to identify potential phishing emails?
- Do the users know how to escalate potential problems?

Identity Management

- Do all accounts require passwords that are difficult to guess?
- Do accounts make use of multi-factor authentication (MFA)?
- Are separate accounts used for privileged access to systems?
- Are privileged actions logged and audited?

Mobile Devices

- Do laptops use whole disk encryption?
- Is the OS patched regularly?
- Do devices have policies to manage the increased risks?
- Is the use of removable media restricted?
- Do all devices have malware protection enabled?

Secure Configuration

- Are the servers patched regularly?
- Do all servers have malware protection enabled?
- Is all remote access software secured properly?
- Are all access attempts logged and audited?
- Are backups made regularly and tested frequently?

Network Security

- Are firewalls blocking traffic in BOTH directions?
- Are high risk ports explicitly blocked and logged?
- Does remote access (e.g., VPN) require MFA?

Cyber Incident Response

More detailed information can be found in NIST SP 800-61 and NIST SP 800-184

Figure 13: Cyber Incident Response Cycle

Preparation

This phase of the response lifecycle is focused on understanding the managed environment, identifying risks and their associated threat and vulnerabilities, and developing response plans which include:

- Incident Thresholds
- Notification Plan
- Initial Action Plan
- Staffing and Resource Plan

Detection and Analysis

This phase of the lifecycle describes the actions that occur when a security incident has been identified according to the criteria set forth in the preparation phase. Here it is important to document:

- Key indicators of compromise
- Who reported the incident?
- When was it first detected?
- Where was it located?
- What is the current impact?
- How far has the attack propagated?

At this point, it is important to initiate the notification plan and request assistance according to the staffing and resource plan.

Containment, Eradication, and Recovery

The response to the incident will include containing the spread of the malware, removing the malware, closing vulnerabilities, and recovering to a "new normal."

Post-Incident Activities

Once the response is complete, the team will need to review all the documentation created and identify lessons learned. These lessons should be incorporated in the next Preparation phase.

Federal Cybersecurity Resources

Cybersecurity and Infrastructure Security Agency (CISA)

CISA is available to receive reports of any security incident as defined by NIST SP 800-61 including: unauthorized access to systems or data, unwanted disruptions or denials of service, or abuse and misuse of systems or data in violation of policy

Operations Desk: (888) 282-0870 central@cisa.dhs.gov

Federal Bureau of Investigations (FBI)

The FBI is available to receive reports of Internet crime including computer intrusions, intellectual theft, identity theft, criminal hacking, etc. and suspected terrorism, threats of violence, sabotage, or foreign intelligence activity

Local Field Offices: fbi.gov/contact-us/field

Internet Crime Complaint Center (IC3): ic3.gov

National Cyber Investigative Joint Task Force: (855) 282-3937

Federal Communications Commission (FCC)

FCC is available to receive reports of Distributed Denial of Service (DDoS) or Telecommunications Denial of Service (TDoS) attacks that negatively impact communications. Communications Common Carriers regulated by the FCC are required to report communications outages in the Network Outage Reporting System.

FCC Operations Center (FCCOC): 202-418-1122, FCCOPS@fcc.gov

FCC Public Safety Support Center (PSSC): fcc.gov/general/public-safety-support-center

US Secret Service Field Offices / Electronic Crimes Task Forces (ECTFs)

The ECTFs are a part of the US Secret Service and are available to receive reports of cyber-crimes against payment card systems and financial information systems

Local Field Offices: secretservice.gov/contact/field-offices

US Immigration and Customs Enforcement Homeland Security Investigations (ICE/HSI)

The HSI is takes reports of cyber-enabled crime including theft of intellectual property, illicit e-commerce, proliferations of arms and strategic technology, and cyber-related smuggling/ money laundering

Tip Line: 866-347-2423, ice.gov/webform/hsi-tip-form

HSI Cyber Crimes Center: ice.gov/cyber-crimes

Common TCP/UDP Ports

Function	Name	Transport	Session Port
Web	HTTP	TCP	80
	HTTP/S	TCP	443
E-Mail	SMTP	TCP	25
	SMTP/S	TCP	465 or 587
	POP3	TCP	110
	POP3/S	TCP	995
	IMAP	TCP	143
	IMAP/S	TCP	993
Remote Access	SSH	TCP	22
	RDP	TCP	3389
	VNC	TCP	5500
VoIP	SIP	UDP	5060
	SIP/S	UDP	5061
	RTP	UDP	5004-5005
	S/RTP	UDP	5004-5005
	STUN/TURN	UDP	3478
	H.323	TCP	1720
Network Services	DNS	TCP/UDP	53
	NTP	UDP	123
	SNMP	UDP	161-162
Authentication	LDAP	TCP	389
	LDAP/S	TCP	636
	RADIUS	TCP	1812
	Kerberos	TCP	88
Potential Security Risks	MyDoom	TCP	1080
	Kazaa	TCP	1214
	Bagle H	TCP	2745
	MyDoom	TCP	3127
	Blaster	TCP	4444
	eMule	TCP	4672
	Napster	TCP	6699
	BitTorrent	TCP	6881-6999
	Bagle B	TCP	8866
	Tor	TCP	9050-9051

Cryptographic Cipher Recommendations

The following recommendations are from NIST 800-131A Rev. 2

Use	Algorithm	Bit Length	Status	PQC*	Alternate
Block Cipher	RC4	40	Disallowed	No	AES
	DES	56	Disallowed	No	AES
	3DES	168	Disallowed	No	AES
	Skipjack	80	Disallowed	No	AES
	AES	128	Recommended	No	
		192	Recommended	No	
		256	Recommended	Yes	
	SM4	128	Recommended	No	
Authenticated Encryption	AES-CCM	128	Recommended	Yes	
	AES-GCM	128	Recommended	Yes	
	AES-eGCM	128	Recommended	Yes	
Hash	MD5	128	Disallowed	No	SHA2-256
	SHA-1	160	Disallowed	No	SHA2-256
	SHA2	224	Avoid	No	SHA2-256
		256	Recommended	No	
		384	Recommended	Yes	
		512	Recommended	Yes	
	SHA-3	256	Recommended	No	
		384	Recommended	Yes	
		512	Recommended	Yes	
	SM3	256	Recommended	No	
Key Agreement	ECKA-EG	256	Recommended	No	
	ECDH	256	Recommended	No	
Signature	RSA	512	Disallowed	No	RSA-3072
		1024	Disallowed	No	RSA-3072
		2048	Avoid	No	RSA-3072
		3072	Recommended	No	
	DSA	256	Recommended	No	
	ECDSA	256	Recommended	No	
Message Authentication Codes	HMAC-MD5	128	Disallowed	No	HMAC-SHA2
	HMAC-SHA1	160	Avoid	No	HMAC-SHA2
	HMAC-SHA2	256	Recommended	No	
TLS	TLS 1.0	40	Disallowed	No	TLS1.2
	TLS 1.1	128	Avoid	No	TLS1.2
	TLS 1.2	256	Recommended	No	
	TLS 1.3	256	Recommended	No	

*PQC = anticipated Post Quantum Computing use

ACKNOWLEDGEMENTS

Cybersecurity and Infrastructure Security Agency (CISA) is grateful to Ross Merlin, who recently retired from the agency. Ross' last assignment was as the Program Manager for the Shared Resources HF Radio Program (SHARES). Prior to his duties with SHARES, Ross served with the CISA Interoperable Communications Technical Assistance Program (ICTAP). Ross was the author, researcher, and staff officer for the original NIFOG, which Department of Homeland Security (DHS) first published in 2007.

Dan Wills, Editor
Robert Hugi, Asst. Editor

CISA also acknowledges the following contributors:

SAFECOM: Chris Lombard, Red Grasso
NCSWIC: Greg Hauser, John Miller
National Public Safety Telecommunications Council (NPSTC): Don Root
Department of Justice (DOJ): Rob Zanger
Federal Bureau of Investigation (FBI): Lorrie Stoltz
Federal Communications Commission (FCC): Brian Marenco, Justin Cain
Federal Emergency Management Agency (FEMA): Laura Goudreau, Ric Wilhelm
National Interagency Fire Center (NIFC-NIICD): Mike Tuominen
United States Coast Guard (USCG): Sonia Kendall, Matt Skahill
State of Arizona: Dale Brown, Morgan Hoaglin
State of Oregon: Rick Iverson
State of Texas: David Abernathy, Tommy Gonzalez, Karla Jurrens
CISCO Tactical Operations Team: Matt Runyan
San Ramon Valley Fire District, California: Chris Suter
Fairfax County Fire, Virginia: Sean Fensterwald
Fire Department of the City of New York (FDNY): Michael Gomez
Harris County, Texas Public Safety Technology Services: Josh Glover
Illinois Urban Search and Rescue (US&R) Task Force 1: Dave Dato
Lake County, Florida Sheriff's Office: Jason Matthews
Mason-Oceana 9-1-1, Michigan: Ray Hasil
Oklahoma County, Oklahoma: John Comstock
Tennessee Emergency Management Agency: John Johnson (ret.)
Texas A&M Task Force 1 US&R: Andrew White, Gary Parker
CISA: Shannon Roberts, Jim Jarvis, Tom Lawless, Jim Lundsted, Bruce Richter, Jim Stromberg, Joe Galvin, Ken Carpenter, Ellie Brasacchio
Naval Information Warfare Center (NIWC): Jason Fox, Rich Mellor, Jeff Dunmire, Ann Cottingham, Pat Kempker, Jeff C. Lee

NOTES

Self-Adhesive 3-1/2" x 4-3/4"label (22827) can be formatted to add additional content.

NOTES

NOTES

NOTES

NOTES

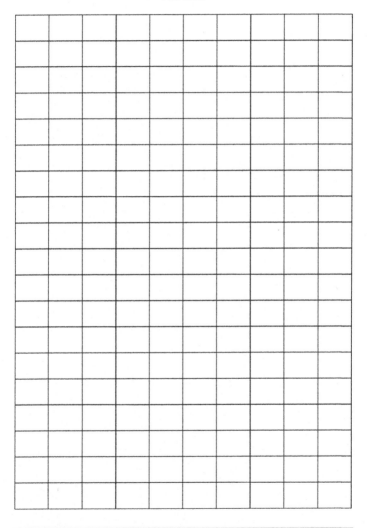

NOTES

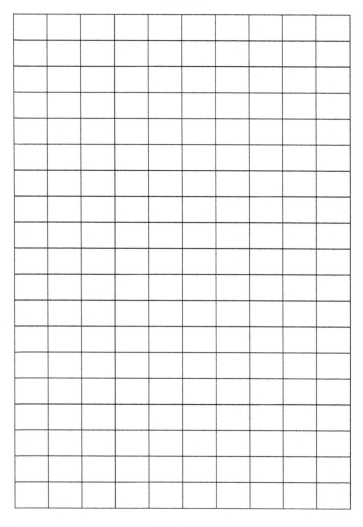

NOTES

NOTES

TIME ZONES

AST	Atlantic Standard
EST	Eastern Standard
CST	Central Standard
MST	Mountain Standard
PST	Pacific Standard
ALST	Alaska Standard
HST	Hawaii-Aleutian Standard
SST	Samoa Standard
ChST	Chamorro Standard
WAKT	Wake Island

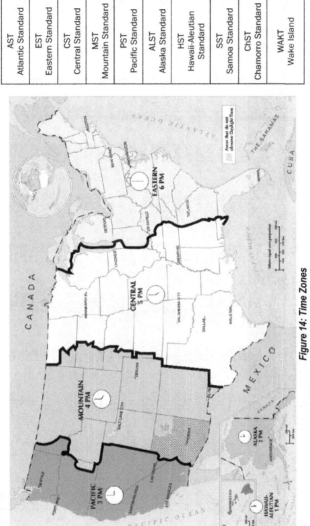

Figure 14: Time Zones

UTC (ZULU) – TIME ZONE CONVERSION CHART

UTC (Zulu) Offset	EDT/AST -4	CDT/EST -5	MDT/CST -6	PDT/MST -7	PST/ALDT -8	ALST -9	HST -10	SST -11	ChST +10	WAKT +12
0000*	2000	1900	1800	1700	1600	1500	1400	1300	1000	1200
0100	2100	2000	1900	1800	1700	1600	1500	1400	1100	1300
0200	2200	2100	2000	1900	1800	1700	1600	1500	1200	1400
0300	2300	2200	2100	2000	1900	1800	1700	1600	1300	1500
0400	0000*	2300	2200	2100	2000	1900	1800	1700	1400	1600
0500	0100	0000*	2300	2200	2100	2000	1900	1800	1500	1700
0600	0200	0100	0000*	2300	2200	2100	2000	1900	1600	1800
0700	0300	0200	0100	0000*	2300	2200	2100	2000	1700	1900
0800	0400	0300	0200	0100	0000*	2300	2200	2100	1800	2000
0900	0500	0400	0300	0200	0100	0000*	2300	2200	1900	2100
1000	0600	0500	0400	0300	0200	0100	0000*	2300	2000	2200
1100	0700	0600	0500	0400	0300	0200	0100	0000*	2100	2300
1200	0800	0700	0600	0500	0400	0300	0200	0100	2200	0000*
1300	0900	0800	0700	0600	0500	0400	0300	0200	2300	0100
1400	1000	0900	0800	0700	0600	0500	0400	0300	0000*	0200
1500	1100	1000	0900	0800	0700	0600	0500	0400	0100	0300
1600	1200	1100	1000	0900	0800	0700	0600	0500	0200	0400
1700	1300	1200	1100	1000	0900	0800	0700	0600	0300	0500
1800	1400	1300	1200	1100	1000	0900	0800	0700	0400	0600
1900	1500	1400	1300	1200	1100	1000	0900	0800	0500	0700
2000	1600	1500	1400	1300	1200	1100	1000	0900	0600	0800
2100	1700	1600	1500	1400	1300	1200	1100	1000	0700	0900
2200	1800	1700	1600	1500	1400	1300	1200	1100	0800	1000
2300	1900	1800	1700	1600	1500	1400	1300	1200	0900	1100

PHONETIC ALPHABET STANDARDS

Standard International		APCO	
A	Alpha	A	Adam
B	Bravo	B	Boy
C	Charlie	C	Charles
D	Delta	D	David
E	Echo	E	Edward
F	Foxtrot	F	Frank
G	Golf	G	George
H	Hotel	H	Henry
I	India	I	Ida
J	Juliet	J	John
K	Kilo	K	King
L	Lima	L	Lincoln
M	Mike	M	Mary
N	November	N	Nora
O	Oscar	O	Ocean
P	Papa	P	Paul
Q	Quebec	Q	Queen
R	Romeo	R	Robert
S	Sierra	S	Sam
T	Tango	T	Tom
U	Uniform	U	Union
V	Victor	V	Victor
W	Whiskey	W	William
X	X-ray	X	X-ray
Y	Yankee	Y	Young
Z	Zulu	Z	Zebra

EMERGENCY MEDICAL PROCEDURES

ICS 206 – Block 8 – "Dutch Creek Protocol"

In the event of a medical emergency, provide the following information to the Incident Communications Center, if established, or appropriate dispatch/coordination center.

1. Declare the nature of the emergency.

    a. Medical injury / illness?

    b. If injury/illness, is it Life Threatening?

2. If Life Threatening, then request that the designated frequency be cleared for emergency traffic.

3. Identify the on-scene Point of Contact (POC) by Resource and Last name (i.e. POC is TFLD Smith).

4. Identify nature of incident, number injured, patient assessment(s) and location (geographic and GPS coordinates).

5. Identify on-scene medical personnel by position and name (i.e. EMT Jones).

6. Identify preferred method of patient transport.

7. Request any additional resources and/or equipment needed.

8. Document all information received and transmitted on the radio or phone.

9. Identify any changes in the on-scene Point of Contact or medical personnel as they occur.